my revisi⏻n notes

AQA A2
BUSINESS
STUDIES

Malcolm Surridge

HODDER
EDUCATION

With thanks to all the students whose valuable feedback helped develop this book.

Hodder Education, an Hachette UK company, 338 Euston Road, London NW1 3BH

Orders

Bookpoint Ltd, 130 Milton Park, Abingdon, Oxfordshire OX14 4SB
tel: 01235 827827
fax: 01235 400401
e-mail: education@bookpoint.co.uk
Lines are open 9.00 a.m.–5.00 p.m., Monday to Saturday, with a 24-hour message answering service. You can also order through the Hodder Education website: www.hoddereducation.co.uk

© Malcolm Surridge 2012
ISBN 978-1-4441-6302-5

First printed 2012
Impression number 5 4 3 2 1
Year 2017 2016 2015 2014 2013 2012

Cover photo reproduced by permission of Valdis Torms/Fotolia

Typeset by Datapage, India

Printed in India

Hachette UK's policy is to use papers that are natural, renewable and recyclable products and made from wood grown in sustainable forests. The logging and manufacturing processes are expected to conform to the environmental regulations of the country of origin.

P02052

Get the most from this book

Everyone has to decide his or her own revision strategy, but it is essential to review your work, learn it and test your understanding. These Revision Notes will help you to do that in a planned way, topic by topic. Use this book as the cornerstone of your revision and don't hesitate to write in it — personalise your notes and check your progress by ticking off each section as you revise.

☑ Tick to track your progress

Use the revision planner on pages 4 and 5 to plan your revision, topic by topic. Tick each box when you have:

- revised and understood a topic
- tested yourself
- practised the exam questions and gone online to check your answers and complete the quick quizzes

You can also keep track of your revision by ticking off each topic heading in the book. You may find it helpful to add your own notes as you work through each topic.

Features to help you succeed

Examiner's tips

Throughout the book there are tips from the examiner to help you boost your final grade.

Typical mistakes

The examiner identifies the typical mistakes candidates make and explains how you can avoid them.

Definitions and key words

Clear, concise definitions of essential key terms are provided on the page where they appear.

Key words from the specification are highlighted in bold for you throughout the book.

Exam practice

Practice exam questions are provided for each topic. Use them to consolidate your revision and practise your exam skills.

Now test yourself

These short, knowledge-based questions provide the first step in testing your learning. Answers are at the back of the book.

Check your understanding

Use these questions at the end of each section to make sure that you have understood every topic. Answers are at the back of the book.

Online

Go online to check your answers to the exam questions and try out the extra quick quizzes at **www.therevisionbutton.co.uk/myrevisionnotes**

My revision planner

Unit 4 The business environment and managing change

Exam practice answers and quick quizzes at **www.therevisionbutton.co.uk/myrevisionnotes**

Countdown to my exams

6–8 weeks to go

- Start by looking at the specification — make sure you know exactly what material you need to revise and the style of the examination. Use the revision planner on pages 4 and 5 to familiarise yourself with the topics.

- Organise your notes, making sure you have covered everything on the specification. The revision planner will help you to group your notes into topics.

- Work out a realistic revision plan that will allow you time for relaxation. Set aside days and times for all the subjects that you need to study, and stick to your timetable.

- Set yourself sensible targets. Break your revision down into focused sessions of around 40 minutes, divided by breaks. These Revision Notes organise the basic facts into short, memorable sections to make revising easier.

Revised ☐

4–6 weeks to go

- Read through the relevant sections of this book and refer to the examiner's tips, typical mistakes and key terms. Tick off the topics as you feel confident about them. Highlight those topics you find difficult and look at them again in detail.

- Test your understanding of each topic by working through the 'Now test yourself' and 'Check your understanding' questions in the book. Look up the answers at the back of the book.

- Make a note of any problem areas as you revise, and ask your teacher to go over these in class.

- Look at past papers. They are one of the best ways to revise and practise your exam skills. Write or prepare planned answers to the exam practice questions provided in this book. Check your answers online and try out the extra quick quizzes at **www.therevisionbutton.co.uk/ myrevisionnotes**

- Try different revision methods. For example, you can make notes using mind maps, spider diagrams or flash cards.

- Track your progress using the revision planner and give yourself a reward when you have achieved your target.

Revised ☐

One week to go

- Try to fit in at least one more timed practice of an entire past paper and seek feedback from your teacher, comparing your work closely with the mark scheme.

- Check the revision planner to make sure you haven't missed out any topics. Brush up on any areas of difficulty by talking them over with a friend or getting help from your teacher.

- Attend any revision classes put on by your teacher. Remember, he or she is an expert at preparing people for examinations.

Revised ☐

The day before the examination

- Flick through these Revision Notes for useful reminders, for example the examiner's tips, examiner's summaries, typical mistakes and key terms.

- Check the time and place of your examination.

- Make sure you have everything you need — extra pens and pencils, tissues, a watch, bottled water, sweets.

- Allow some time to relax and have an early night to ensure you are fresh and alert for the examinations.

Revised ☐

My exams

A2 Business Studies Unit 3

Date: ....

Time: ....

Location: ....

A2 Business Studies Unit 4

Date: ....

Time: ....

Location: ....

1 Functional objectives and strategies

Using objectives and strategies

Functional objectives and corporate objectives

Revised

Corporate objectives

A business's **corporate objectives** could include the following:

- growth — to increase the overall scale of the business
- diversification — looking to sell new products in new markets
- to achieve the maximum possible profits in the long term
- developing innovative goods and services

The setting and communication of clear corporate objectives allows senior managers to delegate authority to more junior employees while maintaining the organisation's overall sense of direction.

> **corporate objectives** — the overall goals of the whole business

Functional objectives

A **functional objective** normally has a numerical element and a stated timescale. For example, a business might set a financial objective which is a specific profit figure in relation to the capital available to the business. The objective will also include a timescale within which it should be achieved.

> **functional objective** — a goal that is pursued by a particular function within the business, such as human resources or marketing

Once clear corporate objectives have been set, it is possible for the business to set objectives at functional levels. The achievement of its objectives by the various functional areas of the business will contribute to the business achieving its corporate objectives. For example, a business that has a corporate objective of growth will require its human resources function to set and achieve objectives to increase the size or productivity (or both) of its workforce, to enable it to increase its supplies of goods or services. At the same time, the finance function may be setting itself goals of increasing the funds available to the business, to allow the objective of growth to be financed fully.

> **Examiner's tip**
>
> When writing about functional objectives, consider how they can impact on other functional areas of the business. This helps to develop analytical arguments and can help you to make and support decisions.

Figure 1.1 Functional objectives and corporate objectives

Functional objectives and functional strategies

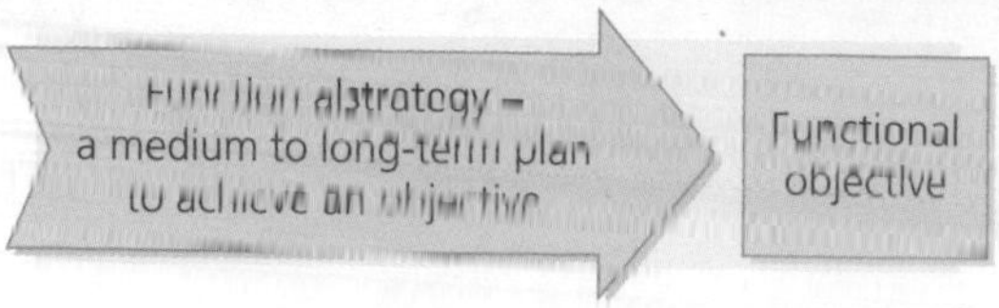

Figure 1.2 Functional objectives and functional strategies

The functional objective should be set first (and should contribute to the achievement of corporate objectives) and then the **functional strategy** should be devised to achieve the functional objective.

Earlier we used the example of a business with a corporate objective of growth, setting a functional objective within the human resources department of developing a larger and more highly skilled workforce. This will require the managers responsible for the human resource (HR) function to devise a strategy to fulfil its functional objectives. The key elements of such a plan may include training employees, recruiting new staff and possibly relocating certain staff.

> **functional strategy** — the medium- to long-term plan used to achieve a functional objective

Typical mistake

Many students do not use the terms 'objectives' and 'strategy' precisely. This weakens their arguments when answering examination questions.

Now test yourself

1 Important corporate objectives include diversification and profit maximisation. For each of these, suggest an appropriate functional strategy for finance, operations, marketing and HR that would help to achieve the relevant corporate objectives.

Answers on p. 106

Check your understanding

1 What is the difference between an objective and a strategy?
2 Explain the distinction between a corporate objective and a functional objective.
3 Why should a corporate objective be set before a functional objective?
4 How might setting clear corporate objectives assist managers in delegating authority within a business?
5 Explain why a corporate objective of innovation might have a significant impact on the functional objectives set by the operations and finance departments in the same business.

Answers on p. 106

2 Financial strategies and accounts

Understanding financial objectives

The nature of financial objectives

Revised

A **financial objective** is a goal or target pursued by the finance department (or function) within an organisation. It is likely that a financial objective will contain a specific numerical element and also a timescale within which it is to be achieved.

There are a number of financial objectives that a business might pursue.

Cash-flow targets

For many businesses, **cash flow** is vital and an essential element of success. Cash flow is the money flowing into and out of a business. Businesses may be growing and need regular inflows of cash to finance the purchase of increasing quantities of inputs such as labour and raw materials. Failure to set financial objectives may result in a business facing financial problems when its expenditure or outflow of cash 'runs ahead' of inflows. Such a situation is described as **overtrading**. Other businesses, such as house builders, have long cash cycles, which mean that a long period of time elapses between starting production and receiving cash from customers. For these businesses, managing cash carefully may be a priority.

Cost minimisation

This financial objective has become better known over recent years due to the publicity given to low-cost airlines and the Easy Group. A financial objective of cost minimisation entails seeking to reduce to the lowest possible level all the costs of production that a business incurs as part of its trading activities. In the case of the low-cost or budget airlines, this has included minimising labour costs, reducing administrative costs by, for example, using the internet for booking, and using 'out of town and city' airports to reduce landing and take-off fees.

Cost minimisation has clear implications for the objectives (and hence strategies) of other functional areas in the business. All functions within the business should aim to operate with minimal expenditure to achieve this financial objective. Cost minimisation is likely to support corporate objectives such as profit maximisation and growth.

Return on capital employed targets

The **return on capital employed** (**ROCE**) is calculated by expressing the operating profits made by a business as a percentage of the value of the capital employed in the business. Stakeholders in a business can compare its current ROCE figure with those achieved by other businesses or with its own figure for previous years. We consider ROCE more fully on p. 17.

> **financial objective** — a goal or target pursued by the finance department (or function) within an organisation

> **cash flow** — the money flowing into and out of a business

> **Now test yourself**
>
> 1 Which of the following two businesses would be more likely to have cash-flow targets as a financial objective: Vickers shipbuilders and engineers, or Greggs the bakers? Why?
>
> Answers on p. 106
>
> Tested

> **Examiner's tip**
>
> Link the functional financial objective to the overall corporate objectives of the business and the objectives set by other functions in the business. In the case of cash-flow targets, the marketing function may set itself objectives such as increasing sales, especially cash sales.

> **Typical mistake**
>
> Many students ignore price elasticity of demand when assessing cost minimisation as a financial objective. Remember, cost minimisation may be more effective in markets where demand is price elastic.

A business might set itself an ROCE target of 20%. This means that its net profits for the financial year will be 20% of the capital employed in the business. This financial objective is very precise and has the advantage of being relatively simple to measure. Achieving such an objective can require actions to increase net profits as well as to minimise the value of assets used within the business.

An ROCE target has considerable implications for other functions. For example, the marketing function may set objectives in terms of market share to improve profitability.

Shareholders' returns

Shareholders' returns is a term that is difficult to define precisely. Some writers take a short-term view and say that it is the current share price and any associated dividends that are due in the near future. Other writers take a longer-term view of shareholders' returns and define it as a combination of short-term returns (both share prices and dividends) as well as future share prices and dividends. In either case, it puts emphasis on generating profits and increasing the value of the company, as reflected in its share price.

Increasing shareholders' returns requires the support of the other functions in the business. Minimising costs can be an important element of any strategy implemented to increase shareholders' returns, and this could have significant consequences for the operations and human resources functions within the business.

> **Examiner's tip**
>
> Remember that a business has stakeholders other than its shareholders. A valid line of argument when tackling questions on shareholders' returns as a financial objective may be to consider the effect on, and reaction of, other stakeholders.

Influences on financial objectives

Revised

The financial objectives that are set and pursued by a business will be influenced by a number of factors, both internal and external. The precise importance of these factors will vary according to circumstances.

Internal factors

Internal factors arise within the business. They include:

- **The corporate objectives of the business.** Arguably this is the most important influence on any financial objective that a business may adopt. A financial objective must assist the business in achieving its overall corporate objectives.

- **The nature of the product that is sold.** If a product's demand is sensitive to price (i.e. if it is price elastic), managers may be more likely to implement and pursue a financial objective of cost minimisation. This financial objective may allow price reduction, with a positive impact on revenue earned.

- **The attitudes and aspirations of the business's senior managers.** If the managers of the business hold large numbers of shares, increasing the shareholders' value might be an attractive proposition, especially if a long-run view is taken of this financial objective. On the other hand, managers may seek the recognition that accompanies growth. In such circumstances, a financial objective of cost minimisation may be more appropriate.

> **Examiner's tip**
>
> Remember that financial objectives are not set in isolation from the rest of the business. They will be part of the creation of corporate objectives as well as the objectives of the remaining functions within the business. These are part of a complementary package.

External factors

External factors arise outside the business. They include:

- **The actions of the business's competitors.** A business will take into account the behaviour of its competitors when setting financial objectives. For example, a business operating in a highly price-competitive market might consider establishing an objective of cost minimisation to allow it more flexibility in pricing decisions.

- **The availability of external finance.** If a business is experiencing difficulty in raising capital, financial objectives are more likely to centre on profits and profitability. Achieving specific returns in terms of profit will reassure potential shareholders or investors.

- **The state of the market.** If the market for the business's products is expanding, it may lead a business's managers to set more expansive financial objectives, such as higher rates of shareholder returns or higher figures for ROCE. In contrast, in a market in which sales figures are stable or declining, financial objectives may be more cautious.

Now test yourself

Tested ☐

2 Construct a table to state one external factor and one internal factor which would encourage managers to adopt each of the four financial objectives set out above.

Answers on p. 106

Using financial data to assess performance

Structure and contents of balance sheets

Revised ☐

The **balance sheet** is an accounting statement of the firm's assets and liabilities on the last day of an accounting period. It can be seen as a 'snapshot' of the firm's current state of affairs at a given time. It lists the assets that the firm owns and sets these against the balancing liabilities — the claims of those individuals or organisations that provided the funds to buy the assets. All businesses have assets and liabilities.

> **balance sheet** — an accounting statement of the firm's assets and liabilities on the last day of an accounting period

Assets

Assets take the form of non-current assets and current assets.

Non-current assets are those assets, such as machinery, equipment and vehicles, which are bought for long-term use (generally more than a year) rather than for resale.

Current assets are items such as inventories (e.g. raw materials) and unsold goods, receivables (money owed by customers), money in the bank and cash. All of these current assets will be converted into cash by the end of the financial year.

Tangible assets are those which exist physically, such as vehicles. In contrast, **non-tangible assets** do not exist in a physical form. An example of a non-tangible asset is a business's trademark, such as Nike's 'tick'.

Liabilities

A business's assets will automatically be matched by its liabilities.

Shareholders' equity or **total equity** is the funds invested in a company by shareholders in order to acquire the assets that the business needs to trade. In the case of businesses other than companies, this may be called **capital** or **owners' funds**. It is a liability because the business technically 'owes' it to the investors.

Non-current liabilities have been borrowed from external sources and will be repaid over the 'long term' (a period longer than 1 year). Examples of non-current liabilities are mortgages, bank loans and debentures.

Current liabilities are debts of the business that will be repaid in the 'short term' (less than 1 year). The most common current liabilities are payables and bank overdrafts.

The assets owned by a business are financed by its liabilities. If all the assets of the business are listed on one side of the balance sheet and all the liabilities of the business are listed on the other, the two totals should balance. This is usually shown vertically, as in Figure 2.1.

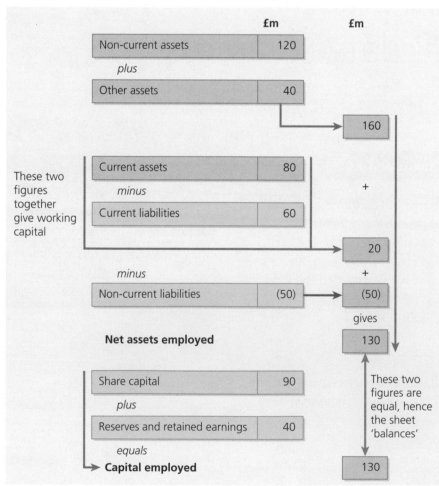

Figure 2.1 The structure of a balance sheet

Exam practice answers and quick quizzes at **www.therevisionbutton.co.uk/myrevisionnotes**

How to analyse balance sheets

- A balance sheet is just a 'snapshot' on one day of the year.
- A key issue is *how* the company has financed the purchasing of its assets. A business may present a stable position, but may face severe problems if it has borrowed heavily and a rise in interest rates occurs.

Balance sheets, working capital and liquidity

Working capital refers to the amount of funds a firm has available for its day-to-day operations. It is the amount of liquid assets that a company has available.

Liquidity measures the extent to which a business is able to pay its short-term debts.

Working capital is an important measure of a business's liquidity and is given by the formula:

working capital = current assets – current liabilities

Working capital is used to pay for the day-to-day running costs of the firm, such as wages, and to finance the purchasing of inventories. It is also used to fund any sales made on credit terms.

Businesses must ensure that they do not have too many current assets in the form of inventories and receivables (that is, people or organisations that owe the business money) as they do not generate profits for the business. But they must make sure that they have enough inventories to meet customer requirements.

If a business has too little working capital available, it may struggle to finance its day-to-day operations. Similarly, if it has too much invested in inventories, it may not be able to afford to purchase new fixed assets.

Liquidity measures two factors:

- **The ability of a firm to meet its short-term debts**, as suppliers' bills and expenses can only be met with cash. Liquidity in this sense measures the company's cash or near-cash equivalents as against short-term debts.

- **The ability of a business to turn its assets into cash.** Cash or near-cash equivalents (e.g. bank deposits) are termed **liquid assets**. Assets that are difficult to turn into cash (e.g. buildings) are termed **illiquid assets**.

Balance sheets and depreciation

Depreciation is the loss in value of a business's assets over time. The amount an asset loses in value each year is a cost to the business. Depreciation is another feature of balance sheets that can be important in analysing the financial performance of the business. Fixed assets have a limited life, even though this could be decades in the case of buildings. Instead of charging the full cost of an asset to the year in which it is bought, it is usual to charge some of the cost to each year of the asset's life. This appears as a charge on the income statement and the process is termed 'depreciation'.

Examiner's tip

It is vital to understand not only the concepts and theories that make up the finance element of the specification, but also their strengths and weaknesses. Many analytical and evaluative questions are set on the uses and drawbacks of the major financial techniques, so this aspect of understanding is particularly worthwhile.

working capital — the amount of funds a firm has available for its day-to-day operations

liquidity — measures the extent to which a business is able to pay its short-term debts

Examiner's tip

This area of finance has close links with the section on liquidity ratios — that is, the current ratio and the acid test ratio — so these are often examined together (see pp. 18–19). The use of ratios such as these will help you to analyse balance sheets more fully.

depreciation — the loss in value of a business's assets over time

When assets are depreciated each year, the amount of the depreciation is included on the income statement as an expense. This means that the amount of the business's profits may be reduced. This is only a 'paper' reduction in profits but has the advantage of reducing the amount of tax that the business has to pay. To avoid this scenario, businesses normally have to work to strict rules imposed by HM Revenue and Customs when calculating deprecation.

Income statements and how to analyse them

Structure of income statements

An **income statement** is an accounting statement that shows a firm's sales revenue generated over a trading period and all the relevant costs incurred in earning that revenue (see Figure 2.2). **Profit** is the difference that arises when a firm's sales revenue is greater than its total costs.

In accounting terms, however, the word 'profit' on its own has little actual meaning. Profit is such an integral objective and such a good indicator of company performance that it is broken down into **gross profit** and **operating profit**.

Gross profit

Gross profit is the measure of the difference between sales revenue and the cost of manufacturing or purchasing the products that have been sold.

gross profit = sales revenue − cost of goods sold

Gross profit is calculated without taking into account costs that could be classified as expenses (e.g. administration, advertising) or overheads (e.g. rent, rates).

It is a useful measure. For example, if company A and company B are providing a similar good or service and company A is making a lower level of gross profit than company B, company A must look closely at its trading position to reduce its expenses and/or overheads.

Operating profit

After calculating gross profit, the next stage is to remove all other expenses and overheads (those costs not directly concerned with the business's trading activities). The result is operating profit.

operating profit = gross profit − (expenses + overheads)

Operating profit is a useful measure. A business may find itself making a healthy gross profit but a small operating profit compared to its competitors. This may be because its overheads are not under control. Calculating both gross and operating profit allows owners/managers to identify problem areas with greater ease.

Finance income and finance expenses

Finance income relates to interest that the business receives on accounts that it holds with banks and other financial institutions. **Finance expenses** are the interest that it pays on loans. Finance income

> **profit** — the difference that arises when a firm's sales revenue is greater than its total costs

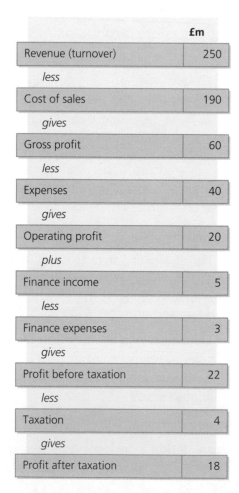

	£m
Revenue (turnover)	250
less	
Cost of sales	190
gives	
Gross profit	60
less	
Expenses	40
gives	
Operating profit	20
plus	
Finance income	5
less	
Finance expenses	3
gives	
Profit before taxation	22
less	
Taxation	4
gives	
Profit after taxation	18

Figure 2.2 The structure of an income statement

and expenses can add to or subtract from a business's operating profit. If its interest received is greater, the difference will be added to operating profit to give a larger figure for profit before taxation. If the interest received is smaller, the net figure will be deducted from operating profit to arrive at profit before taxation.

Profit before and after taxation

All businesses pay tax on profits. Companies pay corporation tax on profits. In 2012 the rate of corporation tax paid by larger companies was cut from 26% to 25%. Once tax has been deducted, we arrive at the final figure on the income statement: profit after taxation for the year.

Analysing income statements

In analysing income statements, the following concepts need to be considered:

- **Profit quality** measures the extent to which an individual profit source is sustainable. A company may make one-off profits from the sale of assets, but these may not be a sustainable source of profits and, if so, will be termed 'low-quality profits'. On the other hand, a company with a strong trading position, which can be expected to make profits in future years, is described as generating 'high-quality profits'.

Profit utilisation

Companies may use profit in two main ways:

- **Retained profits.** These are the share of profits kept by the company and added to the company's balance sheet reserves. Retained profits increase the value of the company, so helping an organisation to expand. A company that retains its profits may perform better in the future.

- **Distributed profits.** These are the portion of a company's profit shared out to external parties, such as owners or partners, preference shareholders and ordinary shareholders.

Now test yourself

3 Write a brief statement to explain the difference between gross profit, operating profit and profit for the year.

Answers on p. 106

Tested

> **profit quality** — measures the extent to which an individual profit source is sustainable

Typical mistake

Do not just consider the size of the profit figure. Profit quality is an important concept to take into account when responding to questions that ask you to consider a company's financial position, and can provide the basis for analysis and judgement.

Financial data and judging performance

Revised

There are a number of issues that you may need to consider when assessing the value of financial data in judging the performance of a business.

The importance of comparisons

It is normally very difficult to make a judgement about a business's balance sheet or income statement without having something to compare it with. There are two main possibilities:

- **The performance of the same business in previous years.** It is helpful to compare the profits or net assets employed for the business for the year before and preferably for several years previously. Most company accounts have 2 years' data for each of the key figures, allowing judgements on whether the trend in the data is improving or not.

- **The performance of similar businesses.** In making judgements consider key figures for other, similar-sized businesses and those that operate in the same industries or markets. You can see whether a particular business holds greater levels of inventories or has recorded or retained greater levels of profit over the last trading year.

Examiner's tip

Objectives provide a yardstick against which to make and support judgements on the financial performance of a business. If, for example, a business has an objective of growth, it may be reasonable to expect lower profits as it invests more in promotion, research and development, etc. Examiners award higher marks for evaluation that is supported.

Taking into account window dressing of accounts

Window dressing is presenting company accounts in such a manner as to enhance the financial position of the company. It is sometimes termed **creative accounting** and involves making modest adjustments to sales, debtors and stock items when preparing end-of-year financial reports.

Important methods of window dressing are as follows:

- **Massaging profit figures.** Surprisingly, it is possible to 'adjust' a business's cost and revenue figures. Following a poor year's trading, the firm might inflate the revenue earned by the business in the final month of trading by including sales from a later period.

- **Hiding a deteriorating liquidity position.** This allows businesses to improve the look of their balance sheets. For example, a business may carry out a sale-and-leaseback deal just prior to accounts being published — this entails selling a major asset and then leasing it back immediately. This increases the amount of cash in the business and makes it look a more attractive proposition for potential investors.

- **Boosting asset values.** Particularly in the area of intangibles, such as brand valuations and goodwill, companies can state the value of assets as being considerably more than their actual worth.

> **window dressing** — presenting company accounts in such a manner as to enhance the financial position of the company

> **Examiner's tip**
>
> An essential means of assessing a business's accounts is through the use of ratio analysis, which we consider in the next section. You should use ratios if you are asked to make judgements about balance sheets and income statements.

Interpreting published accounts

How to conduct ratio analysis   Revised ☐

Ratio analysis is an examination of accounting data through the comparison of two figures. This allows an in-depth interpretation of the data as well as the identification of trends. Ratio analysis measures a number of aspects of a business's performance. In order to analyse the published accounts of businesses, a well-ordered and structured process has to be followed.

Ratios can be classified according to type. They can be used to assess the following aspects of a business's operation:

- profitability
- financial efficiency
- liquidity
- shareholders' ratios
- gearing

Once the reason for the investigation is established, the appropriate range of ratios can be used.

> **Typical mistake**
>
> Many students can calculate ratios successfully but then fail to analyse their answers to say whether the ratios are good or bad in the context of the question.

Types of ratios

Profitability ratios

Profitability ratios measure the relationship between gross/net profit and sales, assets and capital employed. These are sometimes referred to as **performance ratios**.

Gross profit margin

$$\text{gross profit margin (\%)} = \frac{\text{gross profit}}{\text{turnover (sales)}} \times 100$$

Although higher profit margin results are better, any result must be looked at in the context of the industry in which the firm operates. The level of gross profit margin will vary considerably between different markets.

Net or operating profit margin

$$\text{net or operating profit margin (\%)} = \frac{\text{net profit}}{\text{turnover (sales)}} \times 100$$

This measure is used to establish whether the firm has been efficient in controlling its expenses. Again, a higher percentage result is better. It should be compared with previous years' results and with other companies in the same industry to judge relative efficiency. The net profit margin should also be compared with the gross profit margin. If the gross profit margin has improved but the net profit margin has declined, profits made on trading are improving. However, the expenses incurred in running the business are increasing at a faster rate than profits. Thus, efficiency is declining.

Return on capital employed (ROCE)

This is sometimes referred to as the 'primary' efficiency ratio and it is considered to be one of the most important financial ratios. It measures the efficiency of funds invested in the business at generating profits.

$$\text{ROCE (\%)} = \frac{\text{operating profit}}{\text{total equity + non-current liabilities}} \times 100$$

where total equity + non-current liabilities equals capital employed.

Capital employed is the total funds invested in a business. A higher ROCE value is better, since it can provide owners with a greater return. This figure needs to be compared with those of previous years and other firms to make an informed judgement about the performance of the business.

> **capital employed** — the total funds invested in a business

Financial efficiency ratios

Efficiency or activity ratios measure how efficiently an organisation uses its resources. These are sometimes referred to as **asset utilisation ratios**.

Asset turnover

$$\text{asset turnover} = \frac{\text{sales revenue}}{\text{net assets employed}}$$

This ratio measures the efficiency of the use of net assets in generating sales. The figure is normally calculated on an annual basis. An increasing ratio result when compared with previous years indicates increasing efficiency. The business's asset turnover can usefully be compared with those of competitors.

Inventory turnover

$$\text{inventory turnover} = \frac{\text{cost of goods sold}}{\text{average stock held}}$$

This ratio calculates the number of times inventories are sold and replaced. It can only really be interpreted with knowledge of the industry in which the firm operates. For example, if we were examining the accounts of a second-hand car sales business, we might expect it to turn over its entire inventory of cars and replace them with new ones about once a month. Therefore, we would see a result of 12 times. A greengrocer would expect to sell his or her inventories much more frequently.

As a general rule, a higher rate of inventory turnover (and therefore a higher result) is better. The quicker a business is selling its inventories, the quicker it will realise the profit on them.

Debtors' collection period

$$\text{debtors' collection period (days)} = \frac{\text{debtors}}{\text{sales revenue} \times 365}$$

This ratio is designed to show how long, on average, it takes the company to collect debts owed by customers. On public companies' balance sheets, customers who are granted credit are called 'trade receivables', but we shall use the term 'debtors' for this ratio. Generally a shorter period is preferable.

Creditors' collection period

$$\text{creditors' collection period (days)} = \frac{\text{creditors}}{\text{sales revenue} \times 365}$$

This ratio is designed to show how many days, on average, it takes the company to pay its suppliers. On public companies' balance sheets, people and organisations that are owed money by the business are called 'trade payables' but we shall use the term 'creditors' for this ratio. From a business's point of view, it is best to delay payment, if possible, because it improves the liquidity position.

> **Examiner's tip**
>
> Compare the debtors' and creditors' collection periods. If a business takes longer to collect money from debtors (receivables) than it is allowed to pay creditors (payables) then it may encounter problems with its liquidity. Action needs to be taken.

Liquidity ratios

Liquidity ratios investigate the short-term and long-term financial stability of the firm by examining the relationships between assets and liabilities.

Current ratio

$$\text{current ratio} = \text{current assets} : \text{current liabilities}$$

It is generally accepted that an ideal current ratio is approximately 2:1, i.e. £2 of assets for every £1 of debt or liability. This is because some current assets are inventories, which can be difficult to convert into cash. The acid test ratio overcomes this by excluding inventories.

Acid test ratio

$$\text{acid test} = (\text{current assets} - \text{inventories}) : \text{current liabilities}$$

Again, conventional wisdom states that an ideal result for this ratio should be approximately 1.1:1, indicating that the organisation has £1.10 to pay every £1 of debt. The company can therefore pay all its debts and has a 10% safety margin as well. A result below this (e.g. 0.8:1) indicates that the firm may have difficulties meeting short-term payments. Some businesses, however, are able to operate with a very low level of liquidity. Supermarkets, for example, can do so because they do not offer customers credit, and income flows into the business immediately a sale is made.

Shareholders' ratios

This group of ratios, also termed **investment ratios**, is concerned with analysing the returns for shareholders. They examine the relationship between the number of shares issued, the dividend paid, the value of shares and company profits.

Dividend per share

$$\text{dividend per share (in pence)} = \frac{\text{total dividends}}{\text{number of issued ordinary shares}}$$

Dividend yield

$$\text{dividend yield (\%)} = \frac{\text{dividend per share (in pence)}}{\text{market price (in pence)} \times 100}$$

Again, a higher result is better. However, the result would once more need to be compared with previous and competitor results.

Gearing ratio

Gearing examines the relationship between internal sources and external sources of finance; it compares the amount of capital raised by selling shares with the amount raised through loans.

Gearing focuses on the long-term financial stability of an organisation. It measures the proportion of capital employed by the business that is provided by long-term lenders, as against the proportion that has been invested by the owners. In this way, we can see how much of an organisation has been financed by debt. It is given by the formula:

$$\text{gearing (\%)} = \frac{\text{non-current assets}}{\text{capital employed} \times 100}$$

The gearing ratio shows the degree of risk involved in investing in a company. If borrowed funds comprise more than 50% of capital employed, the company is considered to be highly geared. Such a company has to pay interest on its borrowing before it can pay dividends to shareholders or reinvest profits, and it may experience problems borrowing money.

Examiner's tip

You do not need to learn the formulae for these ratios — they will be provided for you as part of the BUSS3 examination paper. Instead you should concentrate on learning which ones to use in different situations.

Now test yourself

Tested

4 Construct a table to show which two ratios you might choose to develop an answer in each of the following situations. Justify your choices.
   (a) judging whether a business should go ahead with a major investment
   (b) assessing a firm's financial success

Answers on p. 106

Value and limitations of ratio analysis

Revised

Ratio analysis is a helpful tool in analysing the published accounts of businesses. Rather than considering a single figure, such as operating profits, ratios compare the figure against something else, such as the value of capital available to the business. This allows more informed judgements about performance.

Ratios also look at the vital aspects of a business's financial performance. Thus they consider not just the business's profitability, but also its liquidity, whether it has borrowed too much and whether it is efficient.

Ratios help all of a business's stakeholders – managers, shareholders, creditors, suppliers and customers – to make judgements. The financial performance of a business can be assessed from these perspectives using ratio analysis.

Although ratio analysis is a powerful tool, it does have several drawbacks:

● It is retrospective — ratio analysis concentrates on past performance and is not forward looking. Changes in factors such as the external environment mean that the results of analysing a firm's history may not prove to be a good guide to future performance.

● Ratio analysis provides no information about non-financial matters, such as the state of the market, the morale of the workforce and the experience of management.

● Ratio analysis does not take into account the effect that inflation may have on reported figures, especially sales.

> **Examiner's tip**
>
> Do consider this topic when writing evaluatively — it may help to make and support a judgement about the value of any ratio analysis that you carry out in an examination.

Selecting financial strategies

Financial strategies available to a business

Revised

A **financial strategy** is a medium- to long-term plan designed to achieve the objectives of the finance function or department of a business.

Raising finance

A business has to consider how it will raise the capital it needs to purchase non-current assets, pay for research and development, buy other companies or implement new marketing plans. There are two major approaches to raising finance:

● **Borrowing.** Some managers may elect to raise substantial sums through borrowing. This can be relatively quick to arrange, especially if the business has non-current assets that can be used as **collateral** against the loan. (Collateral is security for the investor — it can be sold if the business defaults on its payments.) This strategy for raising finance commits the business to regular interest payments, which may mean that it is less attractive to a business that has experienced cash-flow problems.

> **financial strategy** — a medium- to long-term plan designed to achieve the objectives of the finance function or department of a business

> **Examiner's tip**
>
> It is essential that you think about the implications of these financial strategies for other functions within the business. These strategies cannot be implemented independently and, when answering examination questions on this topic, you should not confine yourself to finance.

- **Selling shares.** This method is slower than borrowing and may be expensive. It can also be a difficult proposition if the business's share price is declining. It may also dilute the control that a particular group of shareholders holds in the organisation. However, it does not commit the business to regular interest payments. Instead the managers will be expected to pay a share of the company's profits to the shareholders (called **dividends**) If the company is experiencing low profits, it has the option to reduce its dividend payments.

Implementing profit centres

A **profit centre** is an area, department, division or branch of an organisation that is allowed to control itself separately from the larger organisation. It makes its own decisions, following corporate objectives, and may produce its own income statement. This might be an attractive financial strategy for a number of reasons:

- Allocating costs and profits on a specific area basis allows for more accurate decision making. Businesses can assess how relatively small sections of the organisation are performing and therefore take more informed decisions.

- Decentralised decision making allows areas to make decisions faster and to be more responsive to changes in local conditions.

- Delegated power and authority improves motivation.

A wide range of businesses use profit centres. British Airways operates most of its routes as separate profit centres and Starbucks' coffee shops are organised as separate profit centres.

However, there are a number of disadvantages of using profit centres:

- They can cause rivalry between different profit centres within a business, with centres competing among each other rather than with other businesses.

- Individual centres can become too narrowly focused and lose sight of overall business objectives.

- Performance of individual areas may be adversely or favourably affected by local conditions, making it difficult to analyse and compare.

- The business is likely to have to invest heavily in training to provide staff with the skills necessary to manage more autonomously.

Cost minimisation

This can be classified as a financial strategy as well as a financial objective. Businesses will seek to implement a cost minimisation strategy by implementing a number of possible policies:

- **Minimising labour costs.** This may be important for firms supplying services, as many of them are likely to face wage and salary expenses that are a high proportion of total costs. Therefore cutting labour costs can have a large impact on overall costs of production.

- **Relocating.** Moving to eastern Europe or Asia will assist in reducing labour costs and also overheads such as building costs. However, in the case of manufacturing the production cost advantages may be offset to some extent by increased transport costs.

> **profit centre** — an area, department, division or branch of an organisation that is allowed to control itself separately from the larger organisation

Examiner's tip

Remember that the value of profit centres varies in relation to the type of business. They are more likely to be attractive to a business that operates a large number of discrete sections or branches, such as a retailer.

- **Using technology.** Technology can replace expensive staff for businesses located in high labour cost countries such as the UK. Thus, the low-cost airlines rely heavily on the internet to process bookings for flights and to allow an inexpensive check in procedure for passengers

Cost minimisation has significant implications for the other functional areas of the business. For example, the marketing department will have to develop a marketing strategy based on a low-cost, low-price product.

Allocating capital expenditure

Capital expenditure is spending on new non-current assets such as property, machinery and vehicles. The way in which a business decides to spend its capital can have a significant effect on the operation of its finance department, and also impact on the other functions in the business. Businesses have access only to limited amounts of capital and any expenditure decisions normally have significant opportunity costs.

- **Investing in machinery.** Businesses may opt to do this to reduce labour costs. This approach will involve heavy initial expenditure on capital items but may lead to a reduction in expenditure later. It also offers the potential advantage of increasing the productivity of the business. There are drawbacks, however. The initial costs are high and workers may need retraining in order to operate the technology efficiently.

- **Investing in property.** Some businesses invest heavily in property to enable them to trade effectively or possibly to enhance their corporate image. For example, supermarkets in the UK hold a portfolio of property in high street and out-of-town locations which is essential to enable them to conduct their business effectively. Hotels and restaurants may purchase property in desirable locations to support an upmarket corporate image. Allocating capital expenditure in this way can help the business to attain its overall corporate objectives.

Now test yourself

5 Draw a spider diagram to show the implications for all four functions within a business (finance, marketing, operations and HR) of implementing a strategy of cost minimisation.

Answers on p. 106

Tested

Making investment decisions

How to conduct investment decisions
Revised

Investment decisions involve risk — resources are to be risked in a venture that may (or may not) bring rewards.

In this section, we assume that the business is profit maximising — it will choose the item of equipment that provides the highest return on the initial investment rather than one that is more environmentally friendly.

There are two major considerations when deciding whether or not to invest in a fixed asset:

- the total profits earned by the fixed assets over the asset's useful life
- how quickly the asset will pay off its cost

The process of assessing these factors is called **investment appraisal**. There are three main methods of investment appraisal:

- payback
- average rate of return
- net present value

Payback

Payback simply means the number of years it takes to recover the cost of an investment from its earnings.

payback — the number of years it takes to recover the cost of an investment from its earnings

Example

A machine is bought for £10,000. The purchaser makes an estimate of the additional revenue for each year that will be generated as a result of using the machine. Assume this is £8000 per year.

In this case, the investment will pay for itself in 1.25 years. This is found by using the formula:

payback = number of full years + (amount of cost left/revenue generated in next year)

additional revenue generated in 1 year = £8,000, so amount left to pay = £2,000; revenue generated in next year = £8,000.

So payback = 1 + (2,000/8,000) = 1.25 years.

This technique is quick and simple but it ignores the timing of payments and receipts.

Average rate of return (ARR)

ARR calculates the percentage rate of return on each investment. It uses the formula below:

$$\text{average rate of return} = \frac{\text{average annual profit}}{\text{asset's initial cost} \times 100}$$

where:

$$\text{average profit} = \frac{\text{total net profit before tax over the asset's lifetime}}{\text{useful life of asset}}$$

ARR — calculates the percentage rate of return on each investment

Example

Machine A will make a profit of £200,000 over 5 years and cost £100,000.		
total profit over 5 years	=	£200,000
average annual profit	=	£200,000/5
	=	£40,000
average rate of return	=	$\frac{£40,000}{£100,000} \times 100 = 40\%$

The average rate of return is considered to be more useful than payback because it pays attention to profits, not just revenue. The final figure should be compared with the rate of interest or alternative investments.

Net present value

The average rate of return method fails to take into account that cash now is worth more than cash received in the future. Payback ignores profitability. However, the **net present value** (NPV) approach takes into account profits *and* the timings of payments and receipts.

Discounted cash flow converts future earnings from an investment into their present values. These present values are then added up and the cost of the investment subtracted from the total. What remains (if anything) is the net present value (NPV). NPV must be positive for the investment to be worthwhile.

> **discounted cash flow** — converts future earnings from an investment into their present values

Example

An investor deposits £1,000 in a savings account. In return, the bank pays a rate of interest. If the rate of interest is 10%, at the end of 1 year the investment will be worth £1,100.

After 2 years:	(£1,100 + 10%) = £1,210
And after 3 years:	(£1,210 + 10%) = £1,331

At the end of 3 years, the investor has £1,331 that was only worth £1,000 3 years ago. Looked at in another way, the current or present value of £1,331 in 3 years' time is £1,000. This is because (assuming an interest rate of 10%) the £1,000 can be invested now to be worth £1,331 in 3 years. Discounting tables are available to provide the discounting factors needed in the calculation below.

Example

An investment project costs £6,000. The rate of interest is 10% and the project will yield returns for 5 years of £1,800 per year.

Year	Cash flow × Discounting factors (from table)	=	Present value
0 (now)	6,000 × 1.00	=	(6,000.00)
1	1,800 × 0.909	=	1,636.20
2	1,800 × 0.826	=	1,486.80
3	1,800 × 0.751	=	1,351.80
4	1,800 × 0.683	=	1,229.40
5	1,800 × 0.621	=	1,117.80
	Net present value	=	£822.00

> **Examiner's tip**
>
> Master all of these techniques of investment appraisal, as examination questions may ask you to use a specific approach to conduct a calculation, or provide figures which are the outcome of one of the methods.

If the resulting figure is positive, the investment project is worthwhile. If the result is negative, the project should not be undertaken. A high figure is preferred to a lower one.

Criteria used in making investment decisions

Revised

There are two main criteria that a business may use to make an investment decision:

- **The rate of interest.** Average rate of return and net present value produce figures that can be compared with the rate of interest. The managers of the business will seek a return that is greater than the current and forecast interest rates, if the average rate of return is used. In the event of using NPV, the current interest rate should produce a positive net present value.

- **Other possible investments.** It is perhaps unusual for a business to consider only a single investment proposal. Investment appraisal techniques may be used to compare several competing investments. Thus **opportunity cost** is an important influence here.

Qualitative influences on investment decisions

Revised

As part of their investment decisions, organisations consider other factors, such as the possible effects on industrial relations, the likely reactions of competitors and the impact of the decision on the business's corporate image. Today many businesses that are investing in major projects have to consider the environmental consequences of their decisions. To be seen not to consider such a high-profile factor may constitute an own goal in terms of public relations.

Check your understanding

Tested

1 Distinguish between a financial objective and a financial strategy.
2 State two internal factors and two external factors that may influence a business's choice of financial objectives.
3 Use examples to explain the difference between assets and liabilities.
4 What is meant by the term 'depreciation'?
5 Which ratios would be used to examine a business's financial efficiency?
6 Which ratios would be used to examine a business's liquidity position?
7 What is meant by the term 'profit centre'?
8 Calculate the payback for a vehicle that costs £100,000 and generates £12,500 in additional revenue each year for its business.
9 What is the average rate of return for a machine that generates a profit of £1 million over a 4-year period and costs £2 million to purchase?
10 Explain why a business should not have too much, or too little, working capital.
11 What is profit quality? Why is it important?
12 Why is making comparisons an important part of judging performance using financial data?
13 State what you consider to be the two most significant weaknesses of using ratio analysis.
14 Explain how implementing profit centres as a financial strategy might affect other functions within the business.
15 Explain why net present value can be considered the best method of investment appraisal.

Answers on pp. 106–107

Exam practice

Pizza Dreams plc

Paul Sn.gebrush established Pizza Dreams plc in 1999. It operates 502 takeaway stores across the UK and Ireland, selling pizzas and other simple fast food. It offers a home delivery service. Paul and the other company directors hold large amounts of shares in the business. The company has a financial strategy of cost minimisation.

The company's early growth was spectacular, although it has slowed in recent years. Latterly it has faced tough competition from rivals such as Domino's and prices in the pizza market have been drifting downwards for two years. Pizza sales grew by 7.1% over the last year. A major competitor cut its prices by 5% last year and still achieved an ROCE figure of 18.9%. Demand for pizzas is price elastic: the latest estimate was −1.7.

Below is an extract from the company's accounts.

Financial item	This financial year (£000)	Last financial year (£000)
Sales turnover	50,457	49,899
Operating profit	3,699	3,457
Current assets	4,071	4,002
Current liabilities	3,120	4,325
Non-current liabilities	20,568	19,045
Total equity	16,535	14,210
Total dividends	1,202	990

The company's share price fell from 128 pence last financial year to 120 pence per share this financial year. The number of shares issued has remained constant at 10 million.

Questions

1 Analyse the possible reasons why Pizza Dream plc has implemented a strategy of cost minimisation. [10]

2 Paul says his business is financially successful. To what extent do you agree with his view? (You should use relevant calculations to support your answer.) [18]

Answers and quick quiz online

Online

3 Marketing strategies

Understanding marketing objectives

A **marketing strategy** is the medium- to long-term plan required to achieve a business's marketing objectives. Developing a marketing strategy requires:

- careful analysis of the business's current position
- complete understanding of the business and the market in which it operates
- an assessment of the resources available to the business

> **marketing strategy** — the medium- to long-term plan required to achieve a business's marketing objectives

The nature of marketing objectives   Revised ☐

Marketing strategy entails the setting of **marketing objectives**. Marketing objectives are medium- to long-term targets that may provide a sense of direction to the marketing department and to the whole business. A business may have the following marketing objectives:

- **To maintain or increase market share.** For example, a company might seek to increase market share (as measured by value of sales) from 20% to 25% over the next 3 years. Alternatively, it may decide to introduce a new product to maintain its current market share.

- **To broaden its range of products to improve its market standing.** A company may adopt an asset-led approach by using an existing brand name to develop new products. The Virgin Group is a classic example of this approach.

- **To break into a new market (or market segment).** For example, Microsoft launched Windows Phone 7, in an attempt to break into the lucrative smartphone market.

> **marketing objectives** — medium- to long-term targets that may provide a sense of direction to the marketing department and to the whole business

Influences on marketing objectives   Revised ☐

The precise marketing objectives a firm might set will depend on a variety of factors, the relative importance of which will vary from business to business.

Internal factors

- **The business's corporate objectives.** These are clearly a major determinant, since the achievement of the business's marketing objectives should assist it in achieving its corporate objectives.

- **The size and type of firm.** Large firms possessing high degrees of market power may set more expansive and aggressive marketing objectives. In contrast, new entrants to a market or smaller businesses may be less ambitious in the scope of such objectives.

- **The financial position of the business.** A business that is profitable or has a strong cash-flow position may be able to engage in the necessary market research to allow it to develop marketing objectives that are challenging

- **The possession of a unique selling point (USP).** A business that has a USP may set objectives reflecting an expectation of substantial increases in market share or brand recognition. Having a USP that differentiates allows this to be a more realistic objective.

External factors

- **The business's position in the market.** A dominant business may be able to break into new market segments and build on its existing brand image.

- **The expected responses of competitors.** Whether rivals might match any actions taken to achieve particular marketing objectives can be a major determinant in the objectives that are set. This might be particularly influential when the businesses concerned are of similar size and financial power.

- **The state of the economy.** If the economy is growing slowly or not growing at all, marketing objectives will be more conservative, especially for businesses that sell luxury items.

Examiner's tip

This is a topic on which you could be required to write evaluatively. The marketing objectives set by a business depend upon the type of factors listed above. The key point is that we cannot say with certainty what objectives a firm might set. We need to consider the circumstances of the business and the environment in which it operates.

Now test yourself

1 Construct a spider chart to show the major internal and external influences on Tesco's marketing objectives over the next 2 years.

Answers on p. 107

Tested ☐

Analysing markets and marketing

Reasons for, and the value of, market analysis
Revised ☐

Businesses take major marketing decisions regularly. Such decisions are essential and must be successful if a business is to achieve its marketing objectives. Businesses can take two broad approaches to decision making:

- **Decisions based on hunches or instinct.** It is possible for managers to take major marketing decisions, such as whether to introduce a new product, based entirely on instinct. This means that they conduct little or no research and rely on their knowledge of the market.

- **Scientific marketing decisions.** Many factors influence the markets in which businesses trade. Actions of competitors, consumers, suppliers and governments can all have an impact, as can changes in tastes and fashions. It is important to gather as much evidence as possible and to analyse it before taking major marketing decisions. This is why analysing the market can be so important.

Hunch or instinct might be a valid approach in a market that regularly experiences rapid change, where market research cannot be used effectively. It may also be that in some fashion markets, decisions taken by businesses on the design and format of products can help to shape consumers' tastes.

However, dependence on guesswork is a risky approach because it is entirely possible to be wrong. For example, incorrectly predicting a surge in demand for a product can result in a business having a costly surplus of products. Market analysis is an expensive exercise, but it might be less expensive than making a major error in forecasting consumer demand.

> **Typical mistake**
>
> Do not assume that making marketing decisions on the basis of a hunch is wrong. Sometimes quick decisions made by experienced managers can be highly effective.

Methods of analysing trends

Revised

The analysis of marketing data enables firms to:

- forecast future sales, allowing them to produce sufficient quantities of a product to avoid the accumulation of surplus stocks or unfulfilled orders
- assess consumer reactions to the products they are selling
- estimate the future need for resources such as labour, allowing recruitment or redeployment in advance of changes in demand

Analysing trends: extrapolation

A **trend** is an underlying pattern of growth or decline in a series of data. By establishing whether sales trends, for example, are rising or declining, a firm can plan production to meet the demands of the market fully.

Having an insight into future trends can assist firms in taking correct marketing decisions. **Extrapolation** is a relatively simple technique that can assist forecasting.

Extrapolation analyses the past performance of a variable such as sales and extends the trend into the future. If a firm has enjoyed a steady increase in sales over a number of years, the process of extrapolation is likely to forecast a continued steady rise.

Extrapolation can assist managers in identifying market segments that are likely to experience growth or decline, so they can plan production accordingly. Extrapolation simply extends the apparent trend by eye, as shown in Figure 3.1.

> **trend** — an underlying pattern of growth or decline in a series of data
>
> **extrapolation** — analyses the past performance of a variable such as sales and extends the trend into the future

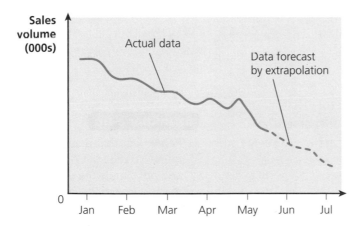

Figure 3.1 The process of extrapolation

However, it may be inaccurate because it assumes that the future will be similar to the past. For this reason, it is not suitable for use in environments subject to rapid change. Predicting that sales of a fashion good, such as clothing, will continue to rise on the basis of extrapolation may be unwise, as a change in fashion may provoke a slump in sales.

Analysing trends: correlation

When analysing market trends, firms will attempt to identify whether there is any **correlation** between different variables and the level of sales. Correlation is a statistical technique used to establish the extent of a relationship between two variables, such as the level of sales and advertising.

Correlation can be illustrated by plotting the two variables against each other on a graph. Figure 3.2(a) plots monthly sales figures against the level of advertising expenditure for the same month. Each month's relationship is shown by an X. It is apparent that higher levels of advertising expenditure lead to higher sales. Managers may be encouraged by this result to increase spending on advertising.

> **correlation** — a statistical technique used to establish the extent of a relationship between two variables, such as the level of sales and advertising

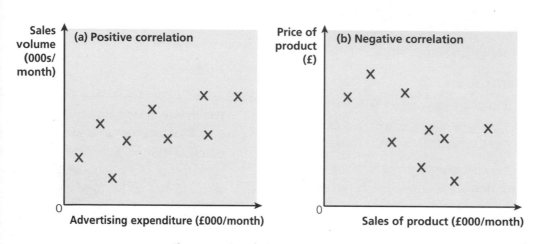

Figure 3.2 Correlation

Figure 3.2(b) shows a negative correlation between the price of a product and its sales. From this managers might decide that demand is price elastic and attempt to reduce the price as far as possible.

Correlation only shows a *possible* relationship between two variables. Sales might rise at the same time as a firm increases its expenditure on advertising. However, the two events might not be related. The rise in sales may be due to a competitor increasing prices or the fact that the firm's products have become fashionable. The results of correlation should be treated with caution.

However, correlation can help to identify key factors that influence the level of sales achieved by a business and assist marketing managers in taking well-informed decisions that are more likely to be accurate.

Analysing trends: moving averages

Moving averages are a series of calculations designed to show the underlying trend in a series of data. They can be calculated over various periods of time, although a 3-year moving average, as shown in Table 3.1, is one of the most straightforward to calculate.

> **Now test yourself**
>
> 2 Write notes to identify two factors that might correlate with sales of suntan lotion in the UK. Would these factors have a positive or a negative correlation?
>
> **Answers on p. 107**
>
> Tested ☐

> **Examiner's tip**
>
> Remember that many factors might influence the sales of a product and not simply the one set out in the correlation. Good analysis and evaluation may centre on a consideration and assessment of these other factors.

Table 3.1 Annual sales of George Ltd, bicycle manufacturers

Year	Bicycle sales	Three-year moving average
2002	1,500	–
2003	1,500	4,500 ÷ 3 = 1,500
2004	1,500	4,650 ÷ 3 = 1,550
2005	1,650	4,725 ÷ 3 = 1,575
2006	1,575	4,820 ÷ 3 = 1,607
2007	1,595	4,870 ÷ 3 = 1,623
2008	1,700	5,100 ÷ 3 = 1,700
2009	1,805	5,270 ÷ 3 = 1,757
2010	1,765	5,470 ÷ 3 = 1,823
2011	1,900	5,545 ÷ 3 = 1,848
2012	1,880	–

In this example the 3-year moving average is calculated by gradually moving down the data, adding 3 years' sales together and dividing the result by 3 to obtain an average annual figure. The average figure is then plotted on the middle year of the three in question. So, for example, the moving average for 2002 to 2004 is plotted next to 2003.

The use of moving averages should smooth out the impact of random variations and longer-term cyclical factors, including seasonal variations, thus highlighting the trend. This can assist managers in taking good-quality marketing decisions, as they can see the underlying pattern of sales for their products.

Now test yourself

3 Calculate the annual moving average for sales of houses using the following data:
2006 — £12.8m, 2007 — £11.6m, 2008 — £11.1m, 2009 — £10.0m, 2010 — £12.2m, 2011 — £13.4m, 2012 — £13.4m.

Answers on p. 107

Tested

How IT can be used in analysing markets

Revised

Information technology (IT) has a range of uses in collecting and analysing marketing data.

Collecting marketing data

It is possible for businesses to use IT as a means of collecting market research data. For example, you might be persuaded to fill in an online survey in return for being entered into a prize draw. IT can collect data on people's spending habits in a variety of ways. Online spending is simple for firms to record and analyse. This can reveal spending patterns of which managers can take advantage. The online retailer Amazon records its customers' purchases and promotes similar products to them at a later date.

A number of supermarkets use loyalty cards. They enable the business to collect data on customers' purchases and to relate them to personal data they have on these customers. Thus, they are able to analyse electronically the types of people who purchase particular products, allowing for better-focused advertising campaigns.

Analysing marketing data

Data that are collected electronically can be analysed and presented using IT. This is a relatively cheap method of data analysis. Data can be analysed in a variety of ways and presented in different formats to ensure that all the messages they contain are understood.

It is possible to argue that in many cases the speed of data analysis afforded by IT may be more of an advantage than its relatively low cost.

Difficulties in analysing marketing data · Revised

Marketing data can give the wrong message for a number of reasons:

- The samples on which the forecasts are based may be too small. This could mean that the views of the sample are not representative of the whole population of consumers.

- Some industries (such as manufacturing mobile phones) are subject to rapid change. Delays between gathering the data and presenting the results to those who take marketing decisions may mean that the market has changed.

- Major changes in the external environment can have substantial effects on the decisions of purchasers. A rise in interest rates, for example, may lead to many consumers delaying or abandoning their decision to purchase, especially if the product in question is bought on credit.

Selecting marketing strategies

Major marketing strategies · Revised

Low cost versus differentiation

One way of thinking about marketing strategies is to consider businesses that base their strategy on being low cost. We have already discussed low-cost financial strategies on pp. 21–22. They offer businesses a way of attracting customers and can be used by businesses that are late entrants to a market and do not have an established brand name. They can be highly effective if demand for the product is price elastic. Airlines such as easyJet have used this marketing strategy to great effect and have captured market share from established airlines. However, the business must have a low cost base and to be able to maintain or reduce its cost levels as established suppliers begin to respond to the challenge.

An alternative approach is to opt for differentiation. This means that a business makes its product distinctive from those of its rivals and gives consumers a reason to purchase it and to become brand loyal. The Co-operative Bank presents itself as ethical and environmental and, using this strategy, has competed successfully against much larger financial organisations.

Ansoff's matrix

A major way to assess a variety of marketing strategies is to use **Ansoff's product–market matrix**, illustrated in Figure 3.3. It assists businesses in evaluating the organisation and the market in which they operate. Developed by Igor Ansoff in 1957, it represents a useful framework for considering the relationship between marketing and overall strategy.

The matrix considers product and market growth, and analyses the degree of risk attached to the range of options open to the business. The key findings of Ansoff's matrix are:

- Staying with what you know (e.g. market penetration) represents relatively little risk.
- Moving into new markets with new products is a high-risk strategy.

Assessment is made of the value of each option.

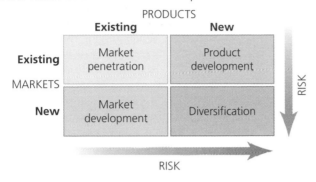

Figure 3.3 Ansoff's matrix

We can look at Ansoff's matrix in more detail.

Market penetration

In this situation, the business's strategy is to market existing products to its existing customers more strongly. By making this choice, the business avoids the commitment in terms of expense and time of developing new products or investigating and analysing unfamiliar markets. This strategy can be implemented relatively quickly and cheaply.

However, it may be that the market is saturated (few, if any, new customers exist), and therefore the only way to increase sales is by taking customers away from competitors. A policy of market penetration in these circumstances can necessitate heavy expenditure on promotion and some flexibility in pricing decisions. Because this marketing strategy does not involve new products or new markets, it is categorised as low risk.

Market development

This strategy involves a business targeting its existing product range at potential customers in a new market. This means that the product remains the same, but it is marketed to a new audience. New markets could be overseas or possibly a different segment within a domestic market. Well-known companies such as Starbucks have engaged in a strategy of market development as they have introduced their products to countries across the globe. One way to achieve market development is through a joint venture with an existing supplier. Tesco has used this approach in China.

This strategy is classified as medium risk because the product or products are unchanged and presumably the business's managers are familiar with their strengths and weaknesses. It also avoids the need for developing new products, which can be costly and time consuming. However, it has drawbacks in that the products may not be accepted in the new markets or they might need expensive modifications if they are to sell in profitable numbers.

Product development

This strategy requires that a new product be marketed to a business's existing customers. The business develops and innovates new product offerings to replace or supplement existing ones. Google continually engages in new product development to stay ahead of its competitors.

The advantages of this approach are that the business knows its customers and is familiar with them already, making market research and subsequent promotion easier. The business may also have a strong brand name that it can attach to its new products as in the case of the Virgin Group. The downside of this strategy is that the business may engage in producing and selling products in which it has limited expertise and it may be vulnerable to the actions of more established businesses in the market. This strategy is categorised by Ansoff as medium risk.

Diversification

This is where a business's marketing strategy is to sell completely new products to new customers. There are two types of diversification: related and unrelated diversification. Related diversification means that a business remains in a market or industry with which it is familiar. An example of this is Virgin moving into rail transport when it already operated Virgin Airlines. Unrelated diversification is where the business has no previous industry or market experience. This took place when Virgin began to produce vodka.

This is a high-risk strategy, as the business lacks experience of the product and the customer base that it is targeting. As a consequence, it will have more chance of making incorrect decisions.

> **Examiner's tip**
>
> The degree of risk involved in these four strategies can be used as a justification for going ahead (or not) with a particular marketing strategy when related to a business's circumstances in a BUSS3 examination.

> **Examiner's tip**
>
> When judging the degree of risk of a strategy of diversification in an examination, look at the financial evidence. What has happened to the company's profits recently and how large is the investment in relation to the company's net assets?

> **Now test yourself**
>
> 4 What factors might encourage a business to opt for a strategy of (a) market development and (b) product development?
>
> Answers on p. 107
>
> Tested ☐

Assessing marketing strategy effectiveness

Revised ☐

The ultimate means of assessing the effectiveness of a particular marketing strategy is to compare it to the business's marketing objectives. If these are fulfilled, the strategy can be deemed to have been successful. A further key means of judgement is to assess the extent to which the marketing strategy has enabled the business to achieve its corporate objectives.

Other measures can also be applied. It may be that a successful marketing strategy will result in other businesses copying it. The first low-cost airline was South West Airlines in the USA. It is a measure of the success of its low-cost strategy that it has been copied throughout the world.

Developing and implementing marketing plans

The major components of marketing plans

Revised ☐

A **marketing plan** is a document setting out the strategy a business will use to achieve its marketing objectives. The plan will include the following:

● Marketing targets that the firm is attempting to achieve.

● The results of the business's market analysis.

- The elements of the marketing mix to be used and how they will be coordinated.
- The timescale to which the plan relates (normally several years).
- The resources available to fund the marketing plan. This section will include a marketing budget.

Marketing budgets

A **marketing budget** is the amount of money that a business allocates for expenditure on marketing activities over a particular period of time. This money is likely to be used for a variety of activities, including advertising, sales promotions and market research.

The size of a firm's marketing budget is determined by a number of factors:

- **The financial position of the business.** If a business is recording rising profits, it is likely to be able to fund higher levels of expenditure on advertising and other marketing activities. However, a business may opt to spend more on marketing at less successful times to increase sales and profits.
- **The actions of competitors.** If a business's rivals are increasing expenditure on marketing activities, many firms will respond to this. For example, the marketing budgets of the businesses competing in the market for package holidays will rise together.
- **The business's marketing objectives.** If a firm has set objectives such as increasing market share, it is likely to spend heavily on marketing. Increasing market share might require substantial expenditure on advertising and sales promotions.

Forecasting sales

Good forecasting is a key component of business success. Firms are likely to want to forecast data that relate to:

- sales of product(s)
- costs for the forthcoming accounting period
- cash flow
- key economic variables, such as inflation, unemployment, exchange rates and incomes

Time-series analysis involves forecasting future data from past figures. A firm is able to predict future sales by analysing its sales figures over previous years. This builds on work we did earlier on analysing trends using techniques such as extrapolation, moving averages and correlation (pp. 29–31).

Analysis of a business's past data can reveal patterns in those data. These patterns may include the following:

- **Trends.** Identifying a pattern in historic data will help the business to predict what will happen in the future. Establishing trends, as shown in Figure 3.4 on p. 36, helps managers to forecast sales and to ensure they have sufficient resources available so that production can meet demand.
- **Seasonality.** This relates to shorter-term fluctuations arising from the time of year. Travel agents expect peak sales in the spring and summer, and costs of vegetables for hotels and restaurants are lower in the summer.

> **marketing plan** — a document setting out the strategy a business will use to achieve its marketing objectives
>
> **marketing budget** — the amount of money that a business allocates for expenditure on marketing activities over a particular period of time
>
> **time-series analysis** — forecasting future data from past figures

Typical mistake

Too many students are unsure about the precise meaning of the term 'marketing plan' and what is included in the plan.

Examiner's tip

When analysing marketing budgets, don't forget that increases here can damage short-term profits and weaken the business's cash-flow position.

● **Cycles.** These reflect periodic changes in patterns over a period of time. It is important for a firm to establish the reasons for these cycles. They may be related to fluctuations in the economy or marketing activities. An example of the operation of cycles is in the building industry, which suffers acutely from economic booms and recessions. In a recession, firms do not want new property, and fewer people purchase new homes.

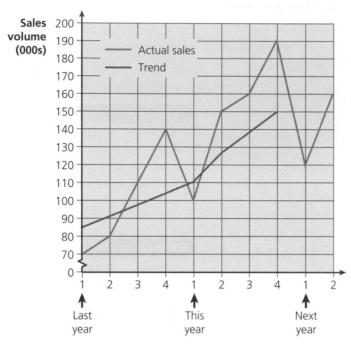

Figure 3.4 Establishing the trend

Why do firms forecast sales?

Businesses might choose to forecast sales for a variety of reasons:

● Sales forecasts form the basis of budgets for many businesses. From these figures, firms can plan production levels and draw up budgets that assist in the management of the enterprise. Sales forecasts also help businesses to predict the timing of income and expenditure, and to express this information in the form of cash-flow forecasts.

● Forecasts help firms to avoid overproduction and the need to sell off inventories at low prices. They also help to avoid unnecessary storage costs.

● Forecasting sales provides important information about changes in the market. If a competitor has introduced a product, or a new business has entered the market, a firm will benefit from an accurate assessment of the impact this change may have on its sales.

> **Typical mistake**
>
> When answering examination questions, students often ignore the factors that influence the importance of sales forecasts. If they are considering a large and expensive project or entering a new and risky market, sales forecasts may be invaluable.

The major influences on marketing plans   Revised

There are a number of key influences on the marketing plan that a particular business may draw up:

● **The finance available to the business.** Access to more funds allows a business to set more expansive and challenging marketing objectives and to pursue them through extensive and expensive advertising campaigns and programmes of new product development.

- **Operational issues.** A business can only put in its marketing plan what it can actually deliver. Thus, the available operational resources will act as a constraint. For example, the productive capacity of the business may determine the number of markets in which it can operate. Additionally, the cost at which the business can supply its products will be a key determinant of its pricing strategy and of the markets in which it thinks it can succeed.
- **Competitors' actions.** It is common for businesses trading in markets that are dominated by a few large firms to consider the likely reactions of competitors as an integral part of planning. In such circumstances, sales forecasts will be drawn up carefully and underpinned with assumptions about the likely responses of rivals. Similarly, the marketing budget will take into account competitors' expected spending levels.

> **Examiner's tip**
>
> Don't forget that marketing plans are subject to influences from all the other functions within the business. A marketing plan should not include what the business cannot afford or what it cannot deliver because of human resources or operational problems.

Issues in implementing marketing plans `Revised`

Marketing planning may be more important for a business that has recently started trading or for one considering a major change, such as entering a new market. A marketing plan may be more valuable for businesses whose markets are not volatile. This means that unexpected changes will not ruin months of careful planning. Despite this, marketing plans do not always work as the planners had intended.

The benefits of marketing planning

- Plans help to give a sense of direction to all employees within the business.
- The business's managers can compare their achievement with the plan and take the necessary action if they are not on target.
- Planning is a worthwhile process in itself. It encourages managers to think ahead and to weigh up the options open to the firm as well as to consider threats and opportunities.

Potential problems in marketing planning

- Drawing up a marketing plan takes time and resources. In a rapidly changing marketplace, this might not be the optimal approach, as quick decisions (possibly based on hunches) might be required.
- Plans might encourage managers to be inflexible and not to respond to changes in the marketplace. Sometimes it might be more important to change the marketing targets than to achieve them.

Check your understanding `Tested`

1 What is the distinction between a marketing strategy and a marketing objective?
2 State two broad approaches that businesses may take to making marketing decisions.
3 Define the term 'extrapolation' and state one weakness arising from its use.
4 A business's sales in five successive years are £4 million, £5 million, £5.2 million, £6.6 million and £7.3 million. Calculate the moving averages for these data.
5 State the four marketing strategies set out in Ansoff's matrix.
6 List the main contents of a business's marketing plan.
7 State one benefit and one potential problem of marketing planning.

8 Explain why diversification is normally considered to be a high-risk marketing strategy.

9 In what ways might a business's marketing objectives influence the size of its marketing budget?

10 In what ways might the actions of a business's competitors influence its marketing plan?

11 Why might businesses use IT to assist in analysing the markets in which they trade?

12 What is the difference between a marketing strategy based on low cost and one based upon differentiation?

Answers on pp. 107–108

Exam practice

Yenix plc

Times have been hard recently for Yenix plc, once a premier retailer of fashion clothes in the UK. The Yenix brand name is still well known and valued in the UK, but some competitors are producing the latest fashions and putting them on sale quickly. The UK market for women's fashion clothing has become saturated.

Yenix plc's profits have declined (by 20% last year to a dismal £12.4 million) and the company appears to have lost its edge in its niche market of women's fashion clothing. Its market share has declined by 15% over 2 years. However, the appointments of a new CEO and a new marketing director have resulted in the development of ambitious plans.

The company has developed a new marketing plan as a result of an extensive programme of market analysis. The key features of its plan are:

- To develop a range of men's fashion clothing to be sold under the Yenix brand name.

- To seek to establish retail outlets in developing countries such as China and Brazil where incomes are rising quickly — there is some recognition in both countries of the Yenix brand.

The company does not wish to engage in a joint venture with foreign retailers as part of its move into the Chinese and Brazilian markets. Instead it intends to appoint staff experienced in these markets to oversee these developments.

Questions

1 Analyse the possible influences on Yenix plc's choice of marketing objectives for the next 3 years. [10]

2 Do you think that the strategy of diversification is the best one in these circumstances? Justify your view. [18]

Answers and quick quiz online

Online

4 Operational strategies

Understanding operational objectives

A business's operations function or department is responsible for the production of the goods or services that the business supplies.

The nature of operational objectives

Revised

Operational objectives are the targets pursued by the operations function or department of the business. The achievement of these goals should assist the business in attaining its corporate objectives. There are a number of operational objectives, the importance of which will vary according to the type of business, and the products that it sells.

Quality targets

A **quality product** is one that meets customers' needs fully. A firm that produces quality products is likely to be a competitive business. A business may set itself several quality targets, such as:

- **A specific percentage of faulty products.** For an insurance company this target could relate to documents with errors, while in a manufacturing context it could be goods that do not operate properly. A business may set a quality target of 1% faulty products, although it is not uncommon for businesses to set targets of zero defects.

- **The implementation of quality standards in a specific timescale.** Businesses may adopt quality standards, most notably ISO 9000. This is intended to assure customers that the business has appropriate procedures for ensuring the supply of quality products.

Cost and volume targets

Cost targets. A **unit cost** is the average cost of producing a single item of output. A business may set itself a **unit cost target**, aiming to produce its products at or below a stated unit cost. Meeting such a cost target allows the business more freedom in its pricing decisions and can increase competitiveness.

Volume targets. These exist when a business plans to produce more than a certain amount of output. For example, a football club such as Tottenham Hotspur may aim for an average attendance in excess of 40,000 per match. This helps to increase market share.

Innovation

Innovation is the creation of new ideas and the successful development of products from these ideas. It can also relate to new ways of making products. A business may set itself a target of being innovative and of bringing a certain number of new products to the market each year.

> **operational objectives** — the targets pursued by the operations function or department of the business

> **Examiner's tip**
>
> Spend a little time looking at your AS Business Studies notes on operations management. These will remind you of many of the concepts, such as quality, that will be covered in detail in this chapter.

> **quality product** — one that meets customers' needs fully

> **unit cost** — the average cost of producing a single item of output

> **Now test yourself**
>
> 1 In what industries might cost and volume targets be important ones for operations management departments? Why?
>
> **Answers on p. 108**
>
> Tested

Innovation is more likely to be an operational target for businesses selling in fashion and technological markets.

Efficiency targets

An **efficient business** produces the maximum number of outputs (goods and services) with the minimum number of inputs (labour, capital and raw materials). Efficiency can take a number of forms.

- **Cost efficiency.** Firms pursuing this objective make products very cheaply, which may be highly attractive to certain groups of customers.
- **Resource efficiency.** Businesses may produce little waste as a consequence of the production process. This may involve recycling off-cuts and any heat or water produced as a by-product.
- **Time efficiency.** Japanese car manufacturers have a record of developing new products more quickly than many of their competitors. Bringing new advanced products to the market early allows them to gain **first mover advantage** and to benefit from a period of **premium pricing**.

Environmental targets

For businesses such as those in the so-called 'polluting sector' (the oil and chemical industries), setting and meeting environmental targets is a vital aspect of effective management. Additionally, retailers (Marks & Spencer, for example) also use environmentally-friendly strategies as a competitive weapon. Environmental targets can take a number of different forms, depending on the nature of the business:

- reducing or eliminating the use of non-sustainable resources
- reducing carbon emissions (the business's 'carbon footprint')
- cutting back on the amount of waste produced in the production process

> **innovation** — the creation of new ideas and the successful development of products from these ideas
>
> **efficient business** — one that produces the maximum number of outputs with the minimum number of inputs

Influences on operational objectives — Revised

Internal influences

The corporate objectives of the business. The corporate and operations objectives of the business should not conflict. For example, a business with a corporate objective of growth may operate with cost targets as prime operational objectives to allow it to reduce prices to increase sales and market share.

The financial position of the business. A business may not be able to afford to invest in machinery to meet self-imposed environmental targets if it is unprofitable.

The nature of the product. For manufacturing firms, environmental issues and therefore targets may be given a higher priority. A business selling a luxury product may set targets in terms of quality; time-based targets may be important in the fashion industry.

External influences

The operations objectives of competitors. Businesses may need to match the operational objectives of their rivals. It would be disadvantageous for one of the UK's major oil companies to be seen to be more damaging to the environment than its competitors.

> **Examiner's tip**
>
> When writing on the influences on the operational objectives set by a business, you will not have time to write about a large number of objectives. Therefore select the most appropriate ones. You will be able to develop these fully and apply them effectively.

Legislation. The UK government and the EU authorities have passed laws that impact on the operational objectives that firms can pursue. Most businesses supplying services are subject to safety laws designed to protect consumers — for example, restaurants are subject to hygiene laws.

Tastes and fashions. A business may set time-based operational targets if it expects regular changes in its customers' tastes and fashions, to enable it to meet their needs promptly.

Scale and resource mix

To operate efficiently it is necessary for a business to operate at the right scale — large enough to benefit from size, but not so large as to become unwieldy. Equally important is to use the right combination of resources of labour and capital.

Economies and diseconomies of scale

Revised

Economies of scale

As firms grow in size, they begin to benefit from economies of scale. **Economies of scale** exist when average or unit costs of production fall as output is increased. This offers businesses huge competitive advantages. Figure 4.1 illustrates this point.

> **economies of scale** — exist when average or unit costs of production fall as output is increased

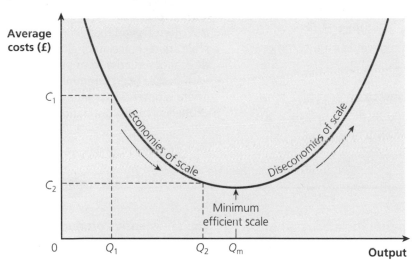

Figure 4.1 Economies and diseconomies of scale

A firm that can only produce an output of $0Q_1$ will face a cost per unit of $0C_1$ and will have to set prices at this level (at least) or face a loss. A larger firm producing $0Q_2$ will be able to price around $0C_2$ and, depending on price elasticity of demand, may dominate the market. One reason why unit costs fall as output expands is that fixed costs are spread over more units of output. Unit costs begin to rise once the firm expands output beyond minimum efficient scale at $0Q_m$.

Economies of scale can take a number of forms.

- **Purchasing economies**, which exist when firms are able to buy components and materials more cheaply, taking advantage of bulk discounts.

> **Examiner's tip**
>
> When considering the benefits of economies of scale, consider **price elasticity of demand**. Economies of scale allow businesses to reduce prices, and by using price elasticity a strong analytical line of argument can be developed.

- **Production economies**, which arise from the use of mass production techniques to speed up production and reduce unit costs.
- **Risk bearing economies**, which mean that larger businesses can afford to take risks when launching new products and even sustain losses to a limited degree.
- **Financial economies**, which mean that larger enterprises can borrow more easily and at more favourable rates of interest, as they have greater reserves.
- **Marketing economies**, which reduce unit costs because firms can afford to advertise extensively — the extra cost is small when spread over many units of output.

Some businesses can benefit more from economies of scale than others. Firms with heavy fixed costs need to produce on a large scale to spread these costs over a large number of units of output and to reduce average costs to a minimum. Similarly, economies of scale are important to businesses in fiercely price-competitive markets.

Diseconomies of scale

Diseconomies of scale are the financial disadvantages that result from producing on a larger scale which result in higher unit costs of production. Large firms can suffer from diseconomies of scale. Once they are past their minimum efficient scale, the cost per unit of production begins to increase. This may be due to:

- **Communication problems.** For example, as the business grows, people may not know whom to report to.
- **Coordination problems.** Managers may experience difficulties ensuring that large numbers of diverse employees pursue common goals.

The fact that large businesses are not necessarily more profitable than small or medium-sized businesses (as measured by ROCE) suggests that diseconomies of scale do operate in the real world.

Now test yourself

2 Identify one business that may benefit from economies of scale and one that may not. Explain your choices.

Answers on p. 108

Tested

diseconomies of scale — the financial disadvantages that result from producing on a larger scale which cause higher unit costs of production

Examiner's tip

It is often argued that economies of scale are technical in origin, while diseconomies arise from problems with people (e.g. communications). There is potential for a powerful line of analysis in this distinction.

Capital and labour intensity

Revised

Capital-intensive production occurs when the production of the good or service relies more heavily on capital (e.g. equipment and machinery) than on other factors of production. Labour-intensive production relies more heavily on the use of labour.

Choosing the resource mix

Deciding on the right mix of labour and capital depends on a number of factors:

- **The size of the business.** A larger firm may be able to afford to use types of technology in its production that a smaller business would not employ. Thus, large-scale car manufacturers such as Nissan rely heavily on computer-controlled robots in production.
- **The type of product.** If a business produces large quantities of standard products, it may be feasible to use a greater proportion of capital in the production process. This would not be a realistic choice for a business producing individually designed products.

capital-intensive production — occurs when the production of the good or service relies more heavily on capital than on other factors of production

- **The finance available to the business.** Adopting capital-intensive production systems can be expensive. The business has to invest in the capital equipment and possibly pay to train its employees to use the equipment, as well as making potential redundancy payments.

Advantages and disadvantages

Labour-intensive production can lead to substantial costs in terms of recruitment, selection and training. This can become a large burden if the business suffers from a high rate of labour turnover. It is also possible that labour disputes will lead to a serious disruption in production. On the plus side, labour-intensive production may allow the business to claim a unique selling point ('handmade' products) and to charge higher prices as demand is more price inelastic.

Capital-intensive production may help businesses to reduce their unit costs and to produce standard goods that meet agreed specifications, including quality targets. Capital-intensive businesses may be more flexible in terms of quantity of output, as the machinery can be operated for longer or shorter periods as desired. However, machinery can be expensive and there is a danger that the technology either is unreliable or becomes obsolescent more quickly than expected.

> **Typical mistake**
>
> Don't assume that capital-intensive production automatically improves quality. It may result in more uniform manufactured products, but these may not meet consumers' needs fully.

Innovation

Innovation and research and development — Revised

Innovation is the creation of new ideas and the successful development of products from these ideas. Innovation can also relate to new ways of making products. **Research and development (R&D)** is scientific investigation leading to new ideas for products and the development of those ideas into products.

Innovation is vital in industries such as pharmaceuticals and consumer electronics, which spend enormous sums of money on developing new products.

> **innovation** — the creation of new ideas and the successful development of products from these ideas
>
> **research and development (R&D)** — scientific investigation leading to new ideas for products and the development of those ideas into products

Purpose, costs, benefits and risk of innovation — Revised

The purpose of innovation

Innovation takes place before a product is launched. This may result in the business facing difficulties with its cash flow. However, a successful business may be able to subsidise new products from more established ones.

When a product enters the growth and maturity stages of the life cycle, firms may invest in innovation for the next generation of products. The purpose of innovation is to give a business a competitive edge. Bringing successful new products onto the market before those of rivals allows a company to develop its reputation and to charge premium prices, thereby boosting profits.

Benefits of innovation

- Businesses can gain a significant competitive advantage by being the first to bring a new product onto the market. A high-technology product with an almost monopoly allows firms to charge high prices (price skimming) and can boost the company's profits.

- Businesses can gain a reputation for producing high-quality and sophisticated products. This image can boost sales of other, related products.

- Patents can be used to protect business ideas for up to 20 years, allowing inventors to generate substantial earnings from their research and innovation.

Disadvantages of innovation

Innovation also has the following costs:

- Research can be very expensive and only large firms can afford to engage in it. Pharmaceutical firms spend millions of pounds developing new products and only a tiny proportion of their ideas result in successful products.

- The timescale can be lengthy, meaning that investors have to wait a long time for a return on their money.

- Other companies may adopt 'me too' products that are similar (but not too similar) to a product resulting from expensive research. These 'me too' products will enjoy some of the sales associated with the original product.

Innovation and risk

There are two main reasons why a strategy of innovation can be risky:

- **The innovative product may fail.** About one in a hundred ideas developed in the pharmaceutical industry actually makes it onto the market. This means that firms spend enormous sums of money on projects that do not generate any returns.

- **Other firms may copy the idea.** This can be a major problem for a business that has incurred all the research and development costs without getting the benefits of selling large numbers of premium-priced products. However, businesses can protect their ideas using patents or copyright.

Location

Methods of making location decisions

Taking location decisions is likely to require the application of important quantitative techniques:

- **Investment appraisal techniques.** Payback, average rate of return and discounted cash-flow techniques may assist managers in taking location decisions. The location that offers the speediest return on the investment, or the greatest return over time, may be selected.

- **Break-even analysis.** Another method of comparison may be to choose the site that requires the lowest level of sales to break even.

Benefits of an optimal location

Revised

Most businesses seek to minimise costs when taking location decisions. Increasingly, location decisions also have an international dimension as companies seek to trade throughout world markets. An optimal location can reduce unit costs in a number of ways:

- **By offering lower labour costs.** This is important for businesses whose labour costs represent a high proportion of total costs.
- **By reducing administrative costs.** There may be fewer laws in some countries with which a business has to comply. This can streamline the production process and reduce costs.
- **By avoiding tariffs (taxes on imports).** Many overseas manufacturers locate in the UK to avoid having to pay tariffs when exporting their products to the EU.

However, optimal locations can offer businesses other benefits too:

- **Access to the latest research facilities.** Some high-technology businesses opt to locate on university research parks, giving the benefit of access to the research facilities.
- **High-calibre staff.** An optimal location can help to attract high-quality staff. Location is not just a question of cost for businesses that require highly trained employees.

Multi-site and international location decisions

Revised

Throughout the developed world, the size of firms is growing, principally through mergers. This means that an increasing number of firms have locations in more than one country. Businesses that operate (as opposed to just selling) in more than one country are known as **multinationals**.

> **multinationals** — businesses that operate (as opposed to just selling) in more than one country

Multi-site location

It is not unusual for large businesses to operate on more than one site. This can be within a single country or in many countries. Many well-known UK businesses (e.g. Waitrose, Barclays Bank) operate many branches. Other businesses (e.g. the Aviva insurance group) operate on a smaller number of larger sites.

Multi-site location creates a number of advantages:

- A multi-site location permits a business to be closer to its markets and to monitor market trends better. Thus, fashion clothing stores that operate throughout the UK can research local markets regularly.
- Some large businesses are in effect several smaller businesses operating as a conglomerate. Having a number of locations allows each element of the business to be in its optimal location.
- Multi-site location encourages a greater degree of delegation and empowerment, which can enhance motivation and employee performance.
- It can allow the firm to operate on a large scale without all the potential problems of diseconomies of scale.

These advantages are balanced to a greater or lesser extent by the disadvantages:

- Communication is more problematic, as employees may be unable to meet face to face.
- The business may incur greater operating costs if materials need to be transported between the various sites.
- With multi-site location the business may be unable to take full advantage of economies of scale. There may, for example, be some duplication of administrative functions, leading to higher costs of production.

International location

International location operates on exactly the same principles as domestic location theory. Multinationals seek the lowest-cost location to maximise profits. Governments often offer incentives, such as grants and benefits, to multinationals for locating in their countries. The UK spends considerable sums of money to attract inward investment into the country.

Multinationals seek the following when taking location decisions:

- effective communications systems and transport networks
- trained and productive labour, available at relatively low rates of pay
- low rates of taxation levied on business profits
- local and national government grants to support the heavy investment necessary

> **Examiner's tip**
>
> Questions on location decisions on BUSS3 are likely to be evaluative. Good-quality answers are likely to be based on all functions within the Unit 3 specification, not just operations management.

Lean production

The concept of **lean production** is increasingly used to describe the organisational goals of manufacturing industry. Lean production describes a range of measures designed to use fewer inputs and resources. The measures include:

- cell production
- just-in-time production
- kaizen or continuous improvement
- benchmarking against market leaders
- time-based management and simultaneous engineering

> **lean production** — a range of measures designed to use fewer inputs and resources

How businesses manage time effectively

Revised ☐

Time-based management

Time-based management seeks to shorten all aspects of production to reduce costs and make it easier to meet the needs of consumers. This type of management requires:

- flexible machinery that can be switched easily and quickly to new models and products

Exam practice answers and quick quizzes at **www.therevisionbutton.co.uk/myrevisionnotes**

- multiskilled employees who can turn their hands to a variety of tasks, reducing delays and production costs
- heavy expenditure on training to ensure employees have up-to-date skills

Lean producers are characterised by short product development times. Having short product development times offers a number of benefits:

- It may prove less costly, as less time and resources are devoted to research and development.
- A firm that is first to launch a product onto the market can engage in price skimming and enjoy higher profits. This is particularly useful if demand is price inelastic.
- The position of market leader in this respect can motivate the workforce, so improving performance and profits.

Simultaneous engineering

Simultaneous engineering manages the development of new products in the shortest possible time. Some aspects of product development can be carried out at the same time, allowing products onto the market faster, cutting costs and generating revenue earlier than would otherwise have been the case.

simultaneous engineering — manages the development of new products in the shortest possible time

Examiner's tip

Remember, the importance of managing time varies according to the type of business. It is an important competitive weapon in industries where products are undifferentiated and similar technology is available to most businesses.

Critical path analysis

Critical path analysis (CPA) is a method of calculating and illustrating how complex projects can be completed as quickly as possible. CPA shows:

- the sequence in which the activities must be undertaken
- the length of time taken by each activity
- the earliest time at which each activity can commence
- the latest times at which each activity must be completed to avoid delaying later activities

critical path analysis (CPA) — a method of calculating and illustrating how complex projects can be completed as quickly as possible

A CPA network consists of two elements, shown in Figure 4.2:

- **Activities.** These, shown by arrows, are the part of a project requiring time and resources. The arrows (running from left to right) show the sequence of the activities. They are given letters to denote the order. The duration of each activity is written below the arrow. Some (but not all) activities cannot be started until others are concluded.
- **Nodes.** These are the start or finish of an activity and are represented by circles. Each node is numbered (in the left-hand segment) and also states the 'earliest start time' (EST) and 'latest finish time' (LFT).

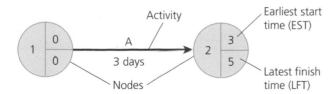

Figure 4.2 Activities and nodes in critical path analysis

An example of critical path analysis

A company is planning to increase capacity by extending its factory. The expansion is expected to cause disruption and the management team is keen to complete it as quickly as possible. The building firm has listed the major activities it will carry out as well as the expected duration of each.

Activity	Expected duration (weeks)
A Design the factory extension	6
B Obtain planning permission	4
C Dig and lay foundations	3
D Order construction materials	2
E Construct walls and roof	12
F Design interior	2
G Install production equipment	6
H Train staff in new techniques	16

The building firm has also provided the following information:

● Activity A is the start of the project.
● B starts when A is complete.
● C, D and F follow B.
● E follows C and D.
● H follows B.
● G follows F.

The network for the factory extension is shown in Figure 4.3.

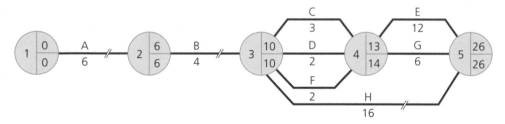

Figure 4.3 The network for the factory extension

The **critical path** shows the sequence of activities that must be completed on time if the whole project is not to be delayed. It is indicated by two small dashes across the relevant activities. In Figure 4.3 the critical path is A-B-H.

Earliest start times and latest finish times

The network in Figure 4.3 shows the earliest start times (ESTs) and latest finish times (LFTs) in the nodes.

● **Earliest start time.** The EST shows the earliest time at which a particular activity can be commenced. ESTs are calculated by working from left to right and adding the times taken to complete the previous activity. If there is more than a single activity, the activity with the longest duration is included in the calculation. The EST is recorded in the top of the two quadrants in the right-hand half of the node. The EST at node 4 is 13 days. This is because although activities D and F are complete after 12 days, activity E cannot commence until both C and D are complete. C is not complete until the end of day 13. The EST on the final node shows the earliest date at which the whole project can be concluded.

● **The latest finishing time.** The LFT records the time by which an activity must be completed if the entire project is not to be delayed.

Exam practice answers and quick quizzes at **www.therevisionbutton.co.uk/myrevisionnotes**

LFTs are calculated from right to left. From each LFT the activity with the longest duration is deducted. The LFT at node 3 is 10 days — the 26 days from node 5 less the 16 days of activity H. Calculating LFTs helps to highlight those activities in which there is some slack time or float.

The critical path

Those nodes in which EST = LFT (i.e. there is no float time) denote the critical path. The critical path:

- comprises those activities that take longest to complete
- allows managers to focus on those activities that must not be delayed for fear of delaying the entire project
- helps managers identify where additional resources might be needed to avoid any possibility of overrunning on projects

Float time

Float time is spare time that exists within a project. Thus, if an activity that takes 5 days has an allowance of 7 days in a network, 2 days of float time exist. In Figure 4.3, if activity E were delayed by 1 day, there would be no impact upon the entire project.

> **Examiner's tip**
>
> In the examination you will not be expected to draw a critical path network from scratch. However, you may have to amend one or to add in LFTs and ESTs. You should therefore ensure that you understand the way in which the networks operate.

The value of critical path analysis

Revised

The value of critical path analysis in any situation depends on the extent to which the advantages outweigh the disadvantages, if they do. The assessment of value needs to be carried out on a case-by-case basis.

Advantages

- CPA encourages managers to undertake detailed planning, which helps to reduce the risk of delays and other problems.
- The resources needed for each activity can be made available at the appropriate time, reducing costs as well as improving the business's cash-flow position.
- Time can be saved by operating certain activities simultaneously. This can be vital in industries where time is an important competitive weapon.
- If delays and problems do occur, the network will assist in working out a solution.

Disadvantages

- Complex activities may be impossible to represent on a network.
- The project still requires management even after the initial network is drawn, as external factors may change.
- Much depends upon how accurately the durations of activities are estimated. These can be difficult to forecast, and if they are wrong, the whole process may be of little value.

> **Typical mistake**
>
> Many students concentrate on the CPA networks and the calculation of ESTs and LFTs. However, do focus on the advantages and disadvantages of key techniques such as critical path analysis. This will help you to write analytically and evaluatively when required.

Other elements of lean production

Revised

The term 'lean production' encompasses a range of techniques that a business may adopt.

Cell production

Cell production divides the activities on the production line into a series of independent units. Each of these units, known as cells, is self-contained. The idea is intended to improve quality and motivation. Each cell should have a team leader supported by multiskilled staff.

Quality is likely to be improved because later cells can become the customers of earlier cells and will reject any substandard items. This imposes a regular and rigorous check on quality and reduces the chance of customers receiving poor-quality products.

Motivation can also be enhanced because employees are given the authority to check their own work to ensure quality. In addition, working in a cell means that employees are involved in producing a complete product (even if it is only a component). Seeing an outcome of their efforts can stimulate workers to improve their performance.

Cell production usually operates alongside the just-in-time approach to production.

Just-in-time manufacturing

Just-in-time (JIT) manufacturing is a Japanese management philosophy that involves having the right items of the right quality in the right place at the right time. JIT is a central component of lean production.

Just-in-time manufacturing is not one technique or even a set of techniques, but an overall philosophy embracing both old and new techniques. The philosophy is based on eliminating waste. Waste means anything other than the minimum level of equipment, materials, parts, space and workers' time. Thus JIT means using the minimum amount of resources to satisfy customer demand.

To comprehend JIT fully, it is important to distinguish between value-added and non-value-added activities in the business:

- **Value-added activities** are those that convert the raw materials and components as part of the manufacturing process. These activities occur on the production line.
- **Non-value-added activities** are those where the raw materials, components or finished products are not being worked on. Examples are storage and repairing faulty products.

Japanese firms employing JIT focus on reducing the time spent on non-value-added activities, thus eliminating waste. It is usual to measure the level of waste in an organisation by measuring inventory levels. High inventory levels tend to hide quality problems, scrap, machine down-times and late deliveries. JIT is designed to highlight such issues.

The key characteristics of JIT are as follows.

- It is based on demand-pull production — demand signals when a product should be manufactured. Use of demand-pull enables a firm to produce only what is required.
- Suppliers of components and other materials must be very responsive to orders from the manufacturer.

> **cell production** — divides the activities on the production line into a series of independent units

> **Now test yourself**
>
> 5 Draw up a table to list the advantages and disadvantages of introducing cell production.
>
> Answers on p. 108
>
> Tested

> **just-in-time (JIT)** — a Japanese management philosophy that involves having the right items of the right quality in the right place at the right time

- It allows a reduction in raw materials, work-in-progress and finished goods inventories. This frees up a greater amount of space in factories.
- The layout of the factory is arranged for the use of multiskilled employees.
- It requires high levels of training to give workers the skills necessary to carry out a variety of tasks.
- Employees engage in self-inspection to ensure that their products are of high quality and that value has been added.
- Continuous improvement is an integral part of JIT.

Kaizen

Kaizen means 'continuous improvement' and is an important element of lean production. It entails continual but small advances in production techniques, each improving productivity a little. Kaizen is the cumulative effect of many small improvements.

The key features of kaizen are as follows:

- Kaizen groups meet regularly to discuss problems and to propose new ideas to improve productivity.
- The improvements proposed under the kaizen system cost relatively little but can have a substantial impact on costs of production.
- Mass production has traditionally relied on larger investments to improve technology. This involves paying for redundancies and large-scale changes also take time to become effective. Lean production invites ideas to produce regular, small improvements in productivity.

The implementation of a policy of kaizen has considerable implications for a business's workforce:

- All employees should be continually seeking ways to improve their performance. This may involve new approaches and techniques, which could be relatively minor.
- Team working is an integral element of continuous improvement. Teams can be the basis of kaizen groups designed to provide ideas and solve problems.
- Empowerment gives employees control over their working lives. Empowered employees will have the authority to propose ideas and to implement their decisions.
- Training is an important component of kaizen. Employees need new skills if they are to fulfil a number of roles within the team.

Inevitably, kaizen has some potential shortcomings:

- Traditional managers may resist its implementation as it reduces their power and control in the organisation.
- The impact of kaizen may diminish over time. This is because the more obvious ideas are implemented early on and because employee enthusiasm may dwindle over time.
- Industries that experience regular changes in consumer tastes and fashions may not be so well suited to kaizen.

Now test yourself

6 List the reasons why a manufacturer of conservatories might opt to use JIT production.

Answers on p. 108

Tested

Kaizen — means 'continuous improvement' and is an important element of lean production

Check your understanding

1 Define the term 'quality'.
2 What is meant by the term 'efficiency'?
3 Give two examples of environmental targets that a business may pursue.
4 What is meant by the term 'innovation'?
5 What is the difference between just-in-time manufacturing and lean production?
6 Distinguish between economies and diseconomies of scale.
7 Explain two factors that may encourage a business to engage in capital-intensive production.
8 Why might an innovative strategy be risky?
9 What are the major benefits of multi-site location?
10 What are the weaknesses of critical path analysis as a management technique?

Answers on pp. 108–109

Exam practice

Zero plc

After 100 years of manufacturing in Bristol, Zero plc is on the verge of a decision to move its factory to Hungary. In recent years the chocolate manufacturer's profit margins have declined (profits last year were down 32% to £101.2 million) and it has encountered occasional cash-flow difficulties. The company's sales in the EU have increased to 67% of production.

Item	UK	Hungary
Average gross wages (£, 2009)	27,903	11,755
Tax rate on profits (%)	20–27	10
Labour productivity (value of average output per hour in £)	27.09	14.91
Average consumption of chocolate per person per year (kg in 2010)	10.3	3.5

The company's plans show that it intends to close its factory in Bristol in stages over a 3-year period as its facilities near Lake Balaton in Hungary are developed. This is a complex project as the company also intends to increase its productive capacity as part of the move. The proposed relocation is forecast to cost £276 million.

The leaking of the company's plans has led to storms of protests from consumer groups, trade unions and Bristol City Council. Some consumer groups have called for a boycott of the company's products by UK consumers.

Questions

1 Analyse the value of critical path analysis to Zero plc in planning its proposed move to Hungary. [10]
2 To what extent do you agree with the company's plans to move its manufacturing capacity to Hungary? [18]

Answers and quick quiz online

5 Human resource strategies

Human resource objectives and strategies

A business's human resource (HR) function or department is responsible for the use of labour within the organisation.

The nature of HR objectives

Human resource objectives are the targets pursued by the HR function or department of the business. The achievement of these goals should assist the business in attaining its corporate objectives. There are a number of HR objectives, the importance of which will vary according to the type of business, its products and the market in which it is trading.

> **human resource objectives** — the targets pursued by the HR function or department of the business

Matching the workforce to the needs of the business

It is normal for the labour needs of a business to change over time. A business might take a decision to produce new products or move overseas. Each of these actions means that the business will require a different workforce. This might require the HR department to recruit new employees, redeploy employees to a new location, or train employees to provide new skills.

Meeting this objective allows the firm to be as competitive as possible because its workforce is the right size and has the required skills.

Making full use of the workforce's potential

A workforce's potential exists in a number of forms:

● **Skills.** It is possible that employees have some hidden skill. For example, a manager might be fluent in a second language. Businesses can use skills audits to identify such skills and then make use of them.

● **Underutilised employees.** Some employees may find that their jobs may not stretch them or utilise their talents fully. Equally, some employees may not have sufficient work to occupy them. Using employees more effectively will improve the performance of the workforce.

● **Overworked or stressed employees.** The opposite circumstance can occur, especially if a business is seeking to reduce its operating costs. This can result in employees having excessive workloads or filling roles for which they are not trained or qualified.

> **Typical mistake**
>
> Students often argue that a business should make more effective use of its workforce, but fail to argue how this should be achieved. Techniques such as training to improve skills and redesigning jobs to improve motivation and productivity would be relevant.

Maintaining good employer–employee relations

Good employer–employee relations offer businesses a range of benefits:

● They make costly strikes and other labour disputes less likely.

● Research has shown that businesses with good industrial relations attract higher-calibre and better-qualified applicants for positions.

● Good employer–employee relations assist a business in maintaining a positive corporate image, which may have a positive effect on sales.

Influences on HR objectives

Revised

Internal influences on HR objectives

● **Corporate objectives.** The objectives set by the HR department must assist the organisation in achieving its overall objectives. If the business has a corporate objective of maximising long-term profits, the HR function might set itself objectives concerned with reducing labour costs.

● **The attitudes and beliefs of the senior managers.** If the senior managers of a business consider the workforce to be a valuable asset, they may want a long-term relationship with employees and are likely to set objectives such as developing the skills of the workforce. Alternatively, they may see employees as an expendable asset to be hired when necessary and paid the minimum rate possible.

● **The type of product.** If the product requires the commitment of a highly skilled labour force (healthcare, for example), making full use of the workforce's skills may be the major objective. However, for businesses selling products produced by machinery and requiring little skilled labour, minimising labour costs may be a key HR objective.

External influences on HR objectives

● **Price elasticity of demand for the product.** When demand for a product is strongly price elastic, it is more likely that a business will opt for HR objectives that allow it to reduce labour costs. This can be seen in the case of budget airlines.

● **Corporate image.** Most businesses will set HR objectives including maintaining good relations with employees. An industrial dispute can be damaging to the image of a business and may lead to a loss in sales.

● **Employment legislation.** The UK government and EU authorities have passed a series of laws designed to protect labour in the workplace. Such laws may encourage businesses to set HR objectives to develop the potential of their workforce, as the law may make it difficult and/or expensive to hire and fire employees.

> **Now test yourself**
>
> 1 How might the following influences affect a business's choice of HR objectives: growth, price-inelastic demand and selling a highly complex product?
>
> **Answers on p. 109**
>
> Tested

The major HR strategies

Revised

Making the most effective use of the workforce has become a strategic function, headed by a senior manager or a director. It also integrates all elements of managing people to ensure that the approach is coordinated.

Not all businesses take the same view of HR strategies. Two broad approaches have emerged (see Table 5.1).

● **'Hard' HR strategy.** The 'hard' HR strategy views employees as a resource to be used as efficiently as possible; they are no different from production machinery. Employees are hired as cheaply as possible, managed closely and made redundant when no longer required.

● **'Soft' HR strategy.** The 'soft' HR strategy is based on the belief that employees are a business's most valuable asset. Thus, it is in

> **Examiner's tip**
>
> Remember that the adoption of a hard or a soft HR strategy by a business has implications for other functions within the business. This can give you important lines of analysis when answering questions in the BUSS3 examination.

Exam practice answers and quick quizzes at **www.therevisionbutton.co.uk/myrevisionnotes**

the business's interest to maximise their value to the organisation. Employees are valued and developed over time and help to make a business more competitive.

Table 5.1 'Hard' and 'soft' HR strategies

	'Hard' HR approach	'Soft' HR approach
Philosophy	Employees are no different from any other resource used by the business.	Employees are the most valuable resource available to the business and a vital competitive weapon.
Timescale	HR management operates in the short term only: employees are hired and fired as necessary.	Employees are developed over a long period of time to help the firm fulfil its corporate objectives.
Key features	• Pay is kept to a minimum. • Little or no empowerment. • Communication is mainly downwards. • Leaders have a Theory X view of employees. • Emphasis is on the short term in recruiting and training employees.	• Employees are empowered and encouraged to take decisions. • Leaders have a Theory Y view of workforce. • Employees are encouraged to extend and update skills. • Employees are consulted regularly by managers. • A long-term relationship is developed with employees through use of internal recruitment and ongoing training programmes.
Associated leadership style	This approach is more likely to be adopted by leaders using an autocratic style of leadership.	This approach is more likely to be adopted by leaders using a democratic style of leadership.
Motivational techniques used	Principally financial techniques with minimal use of techniques such as delegation.	Techniques intended to give employees more control over their working lives, e.g. delegation and empowered teams.

Developing and implementing workforce plans

Components of workforce plans

Revised

A **workforce plan** sets out a business's future labour needs and details how these will be met. Planning the most effective use of human resources is an important element in meeting corporate objectives. Businesses have to decide on the amount and type of labour that they will require, given their objectives and the anticipated level of sales.

Those responsible for HR draw up a workforce plan to detail the number and type of workers the business needs to recruit as well as any necessary redeployments, redundancies and retraining. The plan also specifies how the business will implement its workforce plan.

Businesses require specific information for their development of workforce plans (see Figure 5.1 on p. 56).

> **workforce plan** — sets out a business's future labour needs and details how these will be met

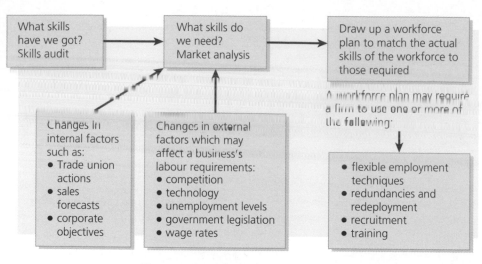

Figure 5.1 Workforce planning

A business's workforce plan will contain the following information:

● Information on the business's current workforce: size, skills, locations and age profile.

● An analysis of likely changes in the demand for the business's products and the business's future labour needs.

● An analysis of the forecast rates of labour turnover for the business and factors affecting the local labour markets.

● Recommendations as to the actions the firm needs to take to acquire and retain the desired workforce.

A workforce plan will allow the company to use its human resources effectively and at minimum cost in pursuit of its corporate objectives.

Now test yourself

2 Construct a flow chart to show the sequence of events necessary to draw up a workforce plan.

Answers on p. 109

Tested

Influences on workforce plans

Revised

There are a wide range of external and internal influences on workforce plans:

● **Sales forecasts.** Estimating sales for the next year or two can help the business to identify the quantity and type of labour the firm will require to meet its expected demand.

● **Demographic trends.** The business also needs information on potential entrants to the labour force, which depends on demographic factors such as migration and birth rates.

● **Wage rates.** If wages are expected to rise, businesses may reduce their demand for labour and seek to make greater use of technology.

● **Technological developments.** Changes in technology may reduce the need for unskilled or even skilled employees, while creating work for those with technical skills.

● **Changes in legislation.** Employment laws can limit the number of hours employees may work each week or require businesses to offer employees benefits such as paternity leave. Such changes may mean that a business requires greater amounts of labour.

Examiner's tip

Sales forecasts are arguably the major influence on a business's workforce plan as they are a vital influence on the quantity and type of labour required.

Issues in workforce planning
Revised

Workforce planning does not take place in a vacuum. HR managers have to take a number of factors into account when drawing up workforce plans:

- **Employer–employee relations.** The business should not take decisions about the workforce without consultation. Indeed, EU legislation makes this a legal requirement for larger businesses. Reducing the size of the workforce through redundancies may result in an industrial dispute, leading to lost sales and the alienation of customers.
- **Changes in technology.** New technology offers businesses different ways to meet the needs of their customers. Bookshops are selling more books using the internet. This has profound implications for workforce plans, as different numbers of employees may be needed for the internet operation, in different locations and with different skills.
- **Human capital.** A business that has appropriately skilled employees who are well rewarded and highly motivated are an asset to the organisation and may offer it a competitive advantage. To make such employees redundant because of a forecast decline in sales may not make sense if this proves to be a short-term decline, or does not occur at all.
- **Migration.** Steady migration into the UK means businesses have access to a substantial source of relatively cheap labour. This contributes to keeping wage rates down in certain occupations, and may have persuaded HR managers to use labour rather than technology in production.
- **Global markets.** Many businesses trade globally and may hire employees from many countries and cultures. This can assist workforce planning by providing a wide range of skills, but may increase communication problems.

The value of workforce planning
Revised

Workforce planning enables managers to have the right employees available in the right place with the right skills. This gives the business a greater chance of meeting the needs of its customers and winning repeat orders. For businesses supplying services, a well-trained workforce can provide a competitive advantage and allow more flexibility in pricing decisions. Managing people effectively is a common feature of successful organisations and is impossible without planning.

Sometimes workforce planning is more difficult and might be of less value. Businesses operating in markets that are subject to wide fluctuations in costs and demand might experience problems in assessing the volume and value of products that they expect to sell and therefore in assessing the quantity and types of labour that they require. The value of workforce planning depends to a significant extent on the accuracy of forecasts of revenues and costs.

Examiner's tip

This is an important element of workforce planning as BUSS3 questions on this topic are likely to be evaluative. This section will help you to think about factors influencing its value, but you must remember to apply this to the scenario in an examination paper.

Competitive organisational structures

Revised

The two main organisational structures businesses may use are:

- functional
- matrix

Functional structures

An organisational structure that is functional is illustrated in Figure 5.2.

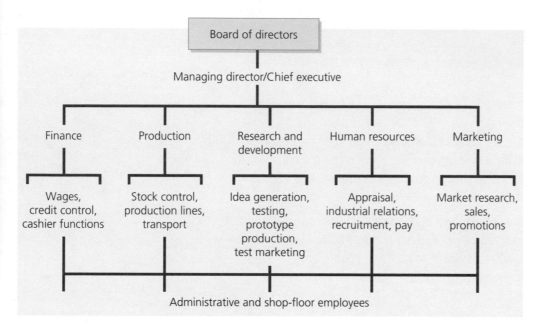

Figure 5.2 A functional structure

The advantages of a functional structure are:

- It allows the business to be coordinated from the top and to have a sense of overall direction.
- It provides clear lines of communication and authority for all employees.
- It lets specialists operate in particular areas, such as marketing and research and development, and to develop new and innovative ideas.

Equally, there are disadvantages of a functional structure:

- Senior managers may become remote as the business grows and may become unaware of local issues.
- Decision making may be slow because of long lines of communication, which may damage competitiveness.
- It provides little coordination and direction to those lower in the organisation.

Matrix structures

The matrix structure (see Figure 5.3) combines the traditional departments seen in Figure 5.2 with project teams. For example, a project team established to develop a new product might include engineers and design specialists as well as those with marketing or financial skills. These teams can be temporary or permanent. Each team member can end up with two or more line managers — their normal departmental manager as well as the manager of the project.

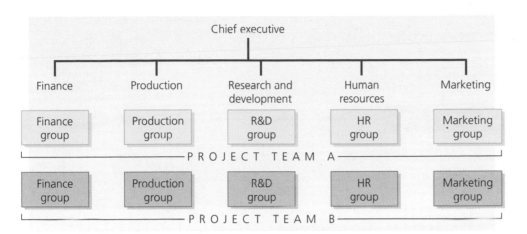

Figure 5.3 A matrix structure

The advantages of a matrix structure are:

- It can help to break down traditional department barriers, improving communication across the entire organisation.
- It can allow individuals to use particular skills in a variety of contexts.
- It avoids the need for several departments to meet regularly, so reducing costs and improving coordination.

The disadvantages are:

- Members of project teams may have divided loyalties, as they report to two or more line managers as well as having heavy workloads.
- There may not be a clear line of accountability for project teams, given the complex nature of matrix structures.

Choice of organisational structure

Revised

- **The environment in which the business is operating.** Fierce competitive pressures may encourage delayering to reduce costs, while rapid change can emphasise the need for a matrix structure to ensure that the organisation remains responsive. The matrix structure would also prevent inflexible hierarchies getting in the way of rapid decision making.
- **The size of the business.** Many small businesses begin with the owner playing a central role. He or she will not be able to sustain this position as the business grows and a large firm is more likely to be organised traditionally, or perhaps as a matrix.
- **The corporate objectives of the business.** An innovative and highly competitive organisation may opt for a matrix structure in order to complete tasks effectively.
- **The culture of the organisation.** If a business has a highly innovative culture, wishing to be a market leader selling advanced products, it may adopt a matrix structure to minimise bureaucracy and to allow teams to carry out the necessary research and development

> **Examiner's tip**
>
> Think about the type of product and the competitiveness and nature of the market in which it is sold when tackling questions on organisational structures. For example, a firm operating in a rapidly changing market such as computer software might benefit from using a matrix structure.

and market research. On the other hand, an organisation that values tradition may be suited to a formal hierarchical structure. This structure places emphasis on positions rather than people and encourages the continuance of existing policies.

Now test yourself

3 Compile a list of the factors that might encourage a business to adopt a matrix structure and those that might encourage it to use a functional hierarchical structure.

Answers on p. 109

Tested

Adapting organisational structures
Revised

Managers can use a number of means of adapting their organisational structures to improve the competitiveness of their businesses.

Delayering

Many businesses in the manufacturing and service sectors have moved towards flatter organisational structures through delayering. **Delayering** involves removing one or more levels of hierarchy from the organisational structure.

Frequently, the layers removed contain middle managers. For example, many high-street banks no longer have a manager in each of their branches, preferring to appoint a manager to oversee a number of branches.

There are a number of advantages of delayering an organisational structure:

- It offers opportunities for delegation and empowerment as the number of managers is reduced and more authority is given to junior employees.

- It can improve communication within the organisation, as messages have to pass through fewer levels of hierarchy.

- It can reduce costs, as fewer employees are required and employing middle managers can be expensive.

Delayering has some potential disadvantages too:

- Not all organisations are suited to flatter organisational structures — large businesses with many low-skill employees may not adapt easily.

- Delayering can demotivate due to job losses, especially if it is just an excuse for redundancies and cost-cutting.

- Initial disruption may occur as people take on new responsibilities and job roles.

- Those managers remaining will have a wider span of control, which may damage communication within the business.

The use of flexible workforces

Flexible workforces are those that are adaptable to changing conditions and demands. A flexible workforce is likely to be multiskilled, well trained and not resistant to change. Performance-related pay may be used to encourage labour flexibility.

Flexible workforces can take a number of forms:

- Some of the workforce may be on **part-time and temporary contracts**, allowing the business to adapt smoothly to changes in the level of demand for its products.

delayering — removing one or more levels of hierarchy from the organisational structure

flexible workforces — those that are adaptable to changing conditions and demands

Now test yourself

4 Explain the circumstances in which delayering is likely to be an effective technique to improve a business's competitiveness.

Answers on p. 109

Tested

- **Core and peripheral workers.** Some businesses employ small numbers of highly skilled core workers and maintain flexibility by employing peripheral workers who may be lower skilled and temporary.

- **Outsourcing.** Some businesses may use other firms to supply part of their output during periods of peak demand.

- Employees may work **flexible hours** through flexitime. This entails employees having to be at work during 'core hours' each day (maybe 10 a.m. until 4 p.m.) and making up the balance of hours at times that suit them.

- Employees may be required to **telework** — to work from home, using computers and other technology to communicate with colleagues and customers. Home working has a similar meaning but may not require the use of technology.

- **Multiskilled employees** are an important element of a flexible workforce. Their ability to switch from one job to another as demand changes, or when colleagues are absent, allows a business to meet the demands of the market more easily and responsively.

The advantages and disadvantages of flexible workforces are outlined in Table 5.2.

Examiner's tip

The notion of competitiveness is an important one and a popular area for questions. For many businesses supplying services, labour forces are an important determinant of competitiveness.

Table 5.2 Advantages and disadvantages of flexible workforces

Advantages	Disadvantages
• Firms can more easily meet fluctuations in demand. • It is simpler to cover for absent staff. • Wage costs may be reduced. • Firms can meet the demand for highly specialised skills relatively cheaply. • Firms can respond rapidly to changing circumstances.	• Communication problems may occur if employees are used irregularly. • Systems such as empowerment and team working may prove difficult to implement. • Lack of security may detract from employee motivation and morale. • A higher turnover of labour may result.

Centralisation and decentralisation

Centralisation occurs when the majority of decisions are the responsibility of just a few people at the top of the organisation. In many senses, centralisation is the opposite of delegation.

Decentralisation occurs when control shifts sideways or horizontally (between people at the same level in the organisation). In contrast, delegation implies a downward shift in control. Decentralisation is not the same as delegation but is often accompanied by it.

Decentralisation offers a range of benefits in terms of giving employees the prospect of greater independence in their working lives, known as **empowerment**, and the motivational benefits that can result from this. Disadvantages of decentralisation are the training costs that might be incurred and the possible loss of a common sense of direction throughout the organisation.

centralisation — when the majority of decisions are the responsibility of just a few people at the top of the organisation

decentralisation — when control shifts sideways or horizontally (between people at the same level in the organisation

Examiner's tip

Delegation is an important element in many examination answers, particularly those requiring analysis and evaluation. It may be a key component of arguments relating to implementation of techniques such as team working and empowerment. It is important to recognise that key AS terms such as delegation have significance for study at A2 level.

Effective employer–employee relations

Communication is the exchange of information between people within and outside organisations. Effective communication systems are important to all businesses. Many managers underestimate the role of communication within a successful organisation. Effective communication can help to maintain good relations between employers and employees.

> **communication** — the exchange of information between people within and outside organisations

Employers are likely to use a number of techniques to communicate with employees, including the following:

- **Meetings.** These include formal meetings with trade unions or other groups representing employees as well as less formal discussions between individual representatives of the two sides.
- **Presentations.** These are frequently used in businesses to explain policies and procedures to large groups of employees.
- **Electronic mail (e-mail).** This method of communication allows computers to speak to one another throughout the world for the cost of a local telephone call. This is particularly useful for quick international communication between employers' and employees' groups across different time zones, as messages can be stored if necessary.
- **Intranets.** These are electronic, computer-based communication networks, similar to the internet but used internally by individual businesses. They are ideally suited to large companies, especially those with a number of locations.
- **Video conferencing.** This allows people to communicate face to face while in different locations, nationally or internationally. It reduces costs and avoids the need for travelling to meetings.

Communication can play an important part in motivating the workforce. Encouraging the views and opinions of all employees will increase their sense of self-worth and should improve motivation. It may also be the source of some good ideas — for example, through quality circles. Such upward communication is a central element in team work and empowerment.

Effective internal communication can help to provide greater understanding of differences in cultures and opinions within an organisation. Employees may take a different perspective on the business and its activities from those of managers. Effective methods of communication will help the two parties to understand each other's viewpoints and may reduce the number of misunderstandings and disputes.

> **Typical mistake**
>
> Many students ignore the importance of communication in fostering good relations between employees and employers. Remember that effective communication can prevent disputes and remove the need for resolution.

Methods of employee representation · · · · · · · · · · · · · · · · · Revised

Trade unions

A **trade union** is an organised group of employees, which aims to protect and enhance the economic position of its members. Trade unions offer a number of advantages to their members:

- negotiation of pay and conditions on behalf of their members, including hours worked and holidays

> **trade union** — an organised group of employees, which aims to protect and enhance the economic position of its members

- protection from unsafe working practices
- improved job security
- a range of associated services, including financial and legal advice

When trade unions negotiate with employers on behalf of their members on matters such as pay, conditions and fringe benefits, this is called **collective bargaining**. They are usually in a better position to negotiate than individuals because they have more negotiating skills and power.

Employers can also benefit from the existence of trade unions for the following reasons:

- They act as a communications link between management and employees.
- Professional negotiation on behalf of a large number of employees can save time and reduce the likelihood of disputes occurring.

In addition to the above functions, trade unions negotiate grievance and disciplinary procedures, and job descriptions and job specifications.

The changing role of trade unions in the UK

Union membership has fallen steadily since 1979, although around 2000 there were signs of a recovery. The decline has occurred because of:

- **Legislation to control the activities of unions.** The Conservative governments of the 1980s and early 1990s passed a series of Acts to limit the impact of unions on business activities. In particular, this legislation made secret ballots on disputes mandatory and restricted the number of pickets.
- **The decline of traditional industries.** Many UK manufacturing industries have declined and employ far fewer people, meaning that the unions associated with them have also become less influential.
- **The increasing number of small businesses.** There has been a rise in the number of small businesses in the UK since the 1980s. These firms are not strongly unionised because they employ few people (and many are part time) and relationships are such that a union is often considered unnecessary.

Other factors, apart from declining membership, have contributed to the declining influence of unions in the UK economy:

- **Single union agreements.** These agreements have been more common since the late 1980s. Under such agreements, employees agree to be represented by one union. This makes negotiation simpler for the employers (as there are only two parties to the discussions) while reducing the possibility of disputes between rival unions. They also assist in developing single status within the organisation and eliminating differences between blue-collar and white-collar workers.
- **Union derecognition.** Some businesses state that they do not wish to recognise unions in the workplace. Although in certain cases this has been a bargaining position in pursuit of means of achieving a single union position, in others the aim has been to eliminate unions from the workplace entirely. However, the Employment Relations Act (2000) has reversed this trend to some extent, as it grants unions the right to recognition as long as they have over 50% of the workforce as members.

Other methods of representation

There are other ways in which employees' views can be represented within the business. **Industrial democracy** gives employees the means of influencing the decision-making processes and of representing their views to employers. Some businesses genuinely attempt to involve employees in decision making, while others implement relevant methods to improve public relations internally and externally.

The main methods of promoting industrial democracy are as follows:

- **Worker directors.** These are shop-floor representatives who are (usually) elected to be members of the board of directors of a business. Unions sometimes oppose the appointment of such directors because other workers may see them as having a hand in implementing unpopular policies, so blurring the distinction between employers and employees. Managers sometimes fear that worker directors may leak sensitive financial information.

- **Works councils.** These are regular meetings between representatives from management and employees. Works councils discuss how to improve the performance of the organisation. Negotiations on pay and conditions are left to other forums.

> **Typical mistake**
>
> When responding to examination questions on employer–employee relations, many students only discuss trade unions. In some circumstances other forms of industrial democracy may be important too.

Avoiding and resolving industrial disputes

Revised ☐

In most cases, disputes can be resolved without trade unions or other employee groups being forced into industrial action. The improvement in industrial relations in recent years has, in part, been a consequence of two main techniques.

Arbitration

Arbitration resolves a dispute by appointing an independent person or panel to decide on a way of settling the dispute. It can take several forms:

- **Non-binding arbitration** involves a neutral third party making an award to settle a dispute that the parties concerned can accept or not.

- **Binding arbitration** means that parties to the dispute have to take the award of the arbitrator.

- **Pendulum arbitration** means that the decision is binding and the arbitrator has to decide entirely for one side or the other. 'Splitting the difference' is not an option. This system avoids excessive claims by unions and miserly offers by employers.

> **arbitration** — resolves a dispute by appointing an independent person or panel to decide on a way of settling it
>
> **conciliation** — a method of resolving individual or collective disputes in which a neutral third party encourages the continuation of negotiation rather than industrial action

Conciliation

Conciliation is a method of resolving individual or collective disputes in which a neutral third party encourages the continuation of negotiation rather than industrial action. The conciliator's role does not involve making any judgement concerning the validity of the position of either party.

Advisory, Conciliation and Arbitration Service

The Advisory, Conciliation and Arbitration Service (ACAS) was set up in 1975 as an independent body with the responsibility to prevent or resolve industrial disputes. ACAS is financed by the government.

ACAS provides employers and employees with arbitration and conciliation services. The organisation also offers other services:

- It advises employers, trade unions and employers' associations on topics such as reducing absenteeism, employee sickness and payment systems.
- ACAS investigates individual cases of discrimination and unfair dismissal.
- It aims to improve business practices to reduce the possibility of industrial disputes.

Check your understanding

Tested

1 Define the term 'human resource objectives' and give two examples.
2 State two internal and two external influences on a business's HR objectives.
3 Explain the difference between a hard and a soft HR strategy.
4 Define the term 'workforce plans'.
5 State two elements of a workforce plan.
6 Outline two techniques a business may use to make its workforce flexible.
7 Explain the difference between centralisation and decentralisation.
8 Explain the difference between arbitration and conciliation.
9 Outline ACAS's main roles.
10 What is 'union derecognition'? Why has this become less common since 2000?

Answers on pp. 109–110

Exam practice

ZZ plc

ZZ plc has an enviable reputation for operating high-quality hotels and 93% of its employees are full time. The company's profits have fallen in recent years with its ROCE hitting an all-time low of 8.8% last year. The company's directors are seeking methods to improve the ROCE figure and have decided to expand the company's portfolio of hotels by buying 16 hotels and offering more competitive prices, while trying to maintain quality. They intend to target tourists in many of the UK's best-known cities and expect demand to be seasonal.

The company's HR director believes that operating a more flexible workforce will assist the company in achieving its objective of increasing ROCE. The company intends to introduce a 'hard' HR strategy for all its operations as soon as possible. Research by the marketing director has shown that the company has achieved a high profit margin but that sales have fallen as demand in the market appears to have become more price elastic over time.

Questions

1 Analyse the possible ways in which ZZ plc may make its workforce more flexible. [10]
2 Do you agree with ZZ plc's decision to implement a 'hard' HR strategy 'as soon as possible'? Justify your decision. [18]

Answers and quick quiz online

Online

6 Corporate aims and objectives

Mission, aims and objectives

The term 'corporate' refers to the entire business, rather than a single function such as marketing.

Mission statements Revised

Mission statements summarise a business's long-term aims and are intended to provide the organisation with a sense of common purpose. Coca-Cola says that its mission is to 'get more people to drink Coke than water'. This reflects its vision to dominate the market.

Mission statements focus on:

- corporate values
- non-financial objectives
- benefits of the business to the community
- how consumers are to be satisfied

Figure 6.1 shows the hierarchy of objectives stemming from a mission statement.

> **mission statements** — summarise a business's long-term aims and are intended to provide the organisation with a sense of common purpose

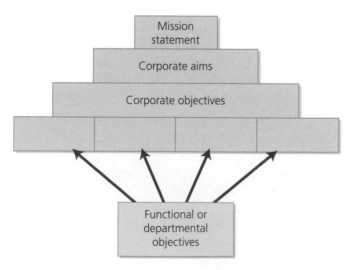

Figure 6.1 The hierarchy of objectives

Corporate aims and objectives Revised

Corporate aims

Corporate aims are long-term plans from which company objectives are derived. They do not normally state targets in numerical terms. From these aims or mission statements, a company can set quantifiable objectives.

Exam practice answers and quick quizzes at **www.therevisionbutton.co.uk/myrevisionnotes**

Corporate objectives

Corporate objectives are medium- to long-term goals established to coordinate the business. Objectives should be quantified and have a stated timescale, such as to earn a 20% return on capital next year. Businesses may have a number of objectives.

- **Survival.** Survival is an important objective during periods of recession or intense competition, or at a time of crisis, such as during a hostile takeover bid.
- **Profit maximisation.** Some firms seek to earn the greatest possible profits to satisfy their shareholders' desire for high dividends. Others are content to pursue a satisfactory level of profit, known as satisficing.
- **Growth.** If a firm grows, it should be able to exploit its market position and earn higher profits. This benefits shareholders (in the long term) by providing greater dividends as well as offering better salaries and more job security to the employees of the business.
- **Corporate image.** This has become a more important objective for many companies recently. Companies fear that consumers who have a negative view of them will not purchase their products.

Which objectives should be pursued?

The objectives pursued by a business vary according to its size, ownership and legal structure. For example, survival might be important to a company during a severe recession, profits to a large public limited company and satisficing to a family-owned private limited company.

> **corporate aims** — long-term plans from which company objectives are derived
>
> **corporate objectives** — medium- to long-term goals established to coordinate the business
>
> **corporate strategy** — the medium- to long-term plan by which a business intends to achieve its corporate objectives

Corporate strategies
Revised

A **corporate strategy** is the medium- to long-term plan by which a business intends to achieve its corporate objectives. The corporate strategy should include:

- the corporate objectives that are being pursued
- the financial and human resources to be used
- the operational resources that will be required to fulfil the plan

If a business has an objective of profit maximisation, it might employ a strategy of innovation or of growth by merger and takeover. The objective can be viewed as the destination for the firm; the strategy is the means to get to the destination.

Different stakeholder perspectives
Revised

Stakeholders are any individuals or groups with an interest in a particular organisation. Stakeholders include:

- managers
- shareholders
- employees
- consumers
- local residents
- creditors
- suppliers

Some of the objectives of stakeholders are common; others are unique to particular types of stakeholder. This is illustrated in Table 6.1.

Table 6.1 Stakeholder objectives

Stakeholder	Likely objectives
Employees	• Job security • High wages • Good working conditions
Shareholders	• Maximum short-term profits • Long-term growth • Positive corporate image
Local residents	• Minimal pollution • Maximum employment • Job security
Suppliers	• Prompt payment • Regular orders • Growth (increasing scale of orders)
Consumers	• High-quality products • Innovative products • Low prices

Some objectives may be supported by a number of stakeholders, whereas others can be more controversial. For example:

- **Maximum short-term profits** might be popular with shareholders, but consumers would oppose this because it might mean high prices, and employees might object because it might mean wages are held down.

- **Social responsibility** involves considering all of society's needs when taking decisions, such as limiting night-time working or building on more expensive brownfield sites as opposed to greenfield sites. These decisions may be supported by local residents and employees, but shareholders could oppose reductions in profits and dividends.

Nowadays, there is much more interest in the idea that firms should fulfil their social responsibilities. Businesses have to consider their actions in the context of a wide range of groups and not just their shareholders.

A number of issues arise from the study of stakeholders and their different perspectives:

- Companies may claim to care about all their stakeholders for purely public relations reasons.

- Even firms that genuinely wish to meet the needs of all stakeholders may find many managers stuck in the previous culture. The change to a stakeholder culture can take years.

Now test yourself

1 Which stakeholders might support a business's move to a cheaper overseas location and which might oppose it? Why?

Answers on p. 110

Tested ☐

Examiner's tip

Do consider the differing viewpoints of stakeholders when responding to questions on the BUSS4 paper. This may assist you in writing analytically and evaluatively.

Check your understanding

Tested ☐

1 What is a 'corporate strategy'?
2 Explain the difference between a corporate objective and a marketing objective.
3 Why is corporate image an important objective for a business operating in a highly competitive market?

Answers on p. 110

Exam practice answers and quick quizzes at **www.therevisionbutton.co.uk/myrevisionnotes**

7 Assessing changes in the business environment

Unit 4 requires you to assess the likely impact of external changes on businesses and to consider the responses that may be made.

Business and the economic environment

Changes in the economic environment can have profound effects on the operation of most businesses.

Level of economic activity

Revised ☐

This refers to the amount of production, expenditure and employment in the economy. A central measure of the level of economic activity is the level of **national income** or **gross national product** (GNP).

The level of economic activity is an important factor in assessing the economic environment in which businesses operate (see Table 7.1). The government tries to manipulate the level of economic activity to provide a positive environment for businesses: for example, by attempting to avoid extreme booms and deep recessions in the trade cycle or periods of high inflation and/or high unemployment.

> **Examiner's tip**
>
> You should relate the theory in Unit 4 to a diverse range of large businesses. You should compare how different businesses respond to similar changes in the economic environment.

Table 7.1 Indicators of rising and falling levels of economic activity

Indicators of rising levels of economic activity	Indicators of falling levels of economic activity
• Increasing output	• Declining levels of production
• Rising expenditure by consumers and businesses	• Falling expenditure by consumers and businesses
• Increasing tax revenue	• Declining tax revenue
• Increasing purchases of imports	• Possible decline in imports
• Greater levels of employment	• Rising unemployment levels
• Build-up of inflationary pressure	• Economic growth slowing and possibly negative
• Economic growth sustained and perhaps increasing	• Possible increase in saving

A number of means are available to the government to alter the level of economic activity in the economy, as shown in Table 7.2. (Government policies are considered more fully on pp. 76–81.)

Table 7.2 Actions to increase and reduce the level of economic activity

Actions to increase the level of economic activity	Actions to reduce the level of economic activity
• Reducing direct taxes, such as income tax	• Increasing rates of direct taxes
• Lowering indirect taxes, such as VAT	• Increasing rates of indirect taxes
• Increasing government expenditure	• Reducing government expenditure
• Implementing policies designed to encourage export sales	• Implementing policies designed to increase savings
• Reducing interest rates	• Increasing interest rates

Now test yourself

1 Explain two benefits to businesses of rises in the level of economic activity in an economy.

Answers on p. 110

Tested ☐

The trade cycle

Revised ☐

The **trade cycle**, also known as the business cycle, describes the regular fluctuations in economic activity occurring over time. Figure 7.1 illustrates the components of a typical trade cycle.

The trade cycle is a major influence on the performance of businesses for two reasons:

● As the economy moves from one stage of the trade cycle to another, businesses can expect to see substantial changes in their trading conditions.

● The government's economic policies are likely to change along with the stage of the trade cycle to compensate for the alteration of the environment in which businesses are operating.

> **trade cycle** — also known as the business cycle, describes the regular fluctuations in economic activity occurring over time

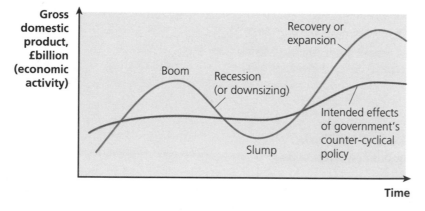

Figure 7.1 The stages of the trade cycle

Figure 7.1 illustrates a smooth and regular trade cycle. In reality, the change in gross domestic product (a measure of national income) is likely to be irregular as economic cycles of different duration and intensity operate simultaneously.

Trade cycles generally have four stages: upswing or expansion, boom, recession and slump, as shown in Table 7.3.

Not all businesses and products are equally affected by the trade cycle. Firms selling luxury products such as antique furniture or foreign holidays are likely to see sales fall as the economy moves into recession. However, retailers of basic foodstuffs and garages selling petrol may remain relatively unaffected.

> **Typical mistake**
>
> Don't write about economic theory when answering questions on this section. Focus on the impact of economic change on businesses and their likely responses.

Table 7.3 Businesses and the trade cycle

Stage of the trade cycle	Possible implications for business	Possible responses of businesses to changing trading conditions
Upswing or expansion	• Rising incomes and expenditures • Possible labour shortages, pushing up wages • Possible rise in output, encouraging expansion	• Opportunity to charge higher prices • Adoption of more technology to replace expensive labour • Decide to invest in fixed assets • Operate nearer to full capacity
Boom	• Possible rise in inflation • Bottlenecks in supply of materials and components • Unable to satisfy levels of demand as consumption rises • Profits likely to be high	• Face increasing pressure to raise prices regularly • Seek methods to increase output (maybe producing at overseas plants) • Offer wage rises to avoid threat of industrial action • Managers plan for falling levels of demand
Recession	• Consumers' disposable incomes start to fall • Demand for many products begins to fall • Some businesses experience financial problems • Excess stocks	• Begin to emphasise price competitiveness in advertising • Seek new markets for existing products • Lay off some workers or ask them to work short time • Possible reduction in trade credit provided
Slump	• Government may initiate counter-cyclical policies, e.g. lower interest rates • Rise in number of bankruptcies • Increased frequency of bad debts • High levels of unemployment	• Offer basic products at bargain prices • Review credit control policies • Continue to target new markets • Seek to diversify product range and sell income-inelastic products • Reduce wage levels

Inflation

Revised

Inflation can be defined as a persistent rise in the general level of prices and a corresponding fall in the value of money. The UK government measures the rate of inflation by using the **consumer price index** (CPI).

Inflation can have a number of adverse effects on businesses:

- Many businesses may suffer falling sales in a period of inflation. Research shows that people save more (perhaps due to uncertainty) and sales for many businesses fall.

- During periods of high inflation, governments or central banks tend to raise interest rates in an attempt to 'cure' the problem. This can lead to a reduction in sales, as consumers are less inclined to borrow money to purchase expensive products.

- It can be difficult to maintain competitiveness (especially international competitiveness) during bouts of inflation. Rising wages and raw material costs may force firms to raise prices or accept lower profit margins. Firms operating in countries with lower rates of inflation may gain an edge in terms of price competitiveness.

- Businesses may experience difficulty in forecasting sales figures and preparing budgets during periods of high inflation.

> **inflation** — a persistent rise in the general level of prices and a corresponding fall in the value of money

> **Examiner's tip**
>
> When writing about the impact of inflation, consideration of price elasticity can prove a valuable line of argument. Firms selling products whose demand is price inelastic are less likely to be affected by rising prices. They can increase prices to maintain profit margins.

Some analysts suggest that low and stable rates of inflation may be beneficial. A steady rise in profits can create favourable expectations and encourage investment by businesses. Inflation can also encourage long-term borrowing by businesses as the real value of their repayments declines over time.

Unemployment

Revised

Unemployment exists when those looking for work cannot find jobs. Governments seek to minimise the level of unemployment because unemployment is a waste of resources, as people willing to work are kept idle.

> **unemployment** — when people looking for work cannot find jobs

Rises in unemployment, actual or forecast, have serious implications for businesses, although the precise impact on firms and their likely responses will depend on circumstances. For example:

- Sales might be expected to fall unless the business is able to sell its products in new markets, perhaps overseas.

- If there is a need to reduce output, then rationalisation and redundancies might follow. Firms may close subsidiary plants. These actions are unlikely to enhance the corporate image of the business.

- Firms generally reduce their levels of inventories during a period of high unemployment in an effort to minimise costs. This can add to the need to reduce current output.

- Research and development plans may be abandoned or postponed, as current levels of demand do not generate enough revenue to finance R&D expenditure.

- The predicted fall in the level of demand may encourage the firm to diversify, particularly into goods and services less susceptible to fluctuations in income. Businesses may consider mergers with other firms to help reduce costs or to broaden product ranges.

If unemployment falls, the effects are reversed.

The precise policies adopted by a firm when faced with changes in unemployment levels might depend on factors such as:

- the organisation's size, financial resources and product range
- the sensitivity of the business's products to changes in income levels
- the ability of the management team and its responses to changing circumstances

> **Now test yourself**
>
> 2 Draw a spider chart to show the possible consequences for a manufacturing business of a significant fall in unemployment.
>
> **Answers on p. 110**
>
> Tested

Interest rates

Revised

The **rate of interest** can be described as the price of borrowed money. The Bank of England's Monetary Policy Committee (MPC) meets monthly to determine interest rates. All other interest rates in the UK economy are based on the rate set by the bank.

> **rate of interest** — the price of borrowed money

Changes in interest rates have significant effects on businesses and the environment in which they operate. They are a central part of monetary policy. For more on this, see p. 78.

Reduced consumer spending

Interest rates affect the level of consumer spending in the economy. A rise in interest rates will normally reduce spending by consumers for a number of reasons:

● Consumers are more likely to take a decision to save during a period in which interest rates are rising. Higher returns will persuade some consumers to postpone spending decisions.

● Rising interest rates increase the cost of borrowing. Many goods are purchased on credit, such as digital televisions. If rates rise, the cost of purchasing these goods on credit will increase, causing falling sales.

● Many UK consumers have mortgages. A rise in interest rates will increase the monthly payments of householders and reduce the income available for other expenditure.

A fall in interest rates will tend to increase demand for many products and expenditure will rise. The reverse of the above will take place.

Higher overheads

A rise in interest rates will result in higher overheads for most businesses. When faced with higher interest rates, firms might limit short-term borrowing but may be able to do little about the increased costs of long-term loans.

Postponed investment

Firms may postpone investment decisions at a time of rising interest rates. The cost of borrowing money to finance any project is likely to increase when rates rise, and investments may then become unprofitable. Postponement of investment decisions reduces the level of economic activity in the economy.

Higher exchange rate

A rise in the UK's rate of interest increases the exchange value of the pound sterling. As interest rates rise in relation to the rates available in other countries, the UK becomes an increasingly attractive target for international investment. Foreigners with money to invest are tempted by the high returns available from UK institutions. However, in order to invest in the UK, foreigners need to purchase pounds. This rise in demand for pounds results in a rise in the exchange rate of the pound. If interest rates fall, the same mechanism operates in reverse (see Table 7.4).

> **Examiner's tip**
>
> Remember that some businesses may benefit during a period of rising interest rates. For example, firms supplying second-hand cars might experience rising sales.

> **Now test yourself**
>
> 3 Construct a flow chart to illustrate the probable effects of a rise in interest rates on the sales of exports by UK firms.
>
> **Answers on p. 110**
>
> Tested ☐

Table 7.4 Effects of a rise or fall in UK interest rates on the value of the pound

If UK interest rates fall...	If UK interest rates rise...
● Foreign investors judge the UK to be a less rewarding place in which to invest their money.	● The UK appears a relatively rewarding location for foreign investors to place their funds.
● They decide to withdraw existing investments and/or not to make new ones.	● Foreign investors decide to invest in UK financial institutions to earn the high rate of interest.
● They sell pounds to purchase the currencies of the countries in which they will now invest their funds.	● They sell their own currencies to purchase pounds in order to be able to invest in the UK.
● The supply of pounds on to the international currency market increases.	● The demand for pounds increases on the international currency markets.
● The exchange value of the pound falls against other major currencies.	● The exchange value of the pound rises against other major currencies.

Exchange rates

An **exchange rate** is the price of one currency expressed in terms of another. So, at the time of writing, £1 is worth US$1.60 or €1.09.

Changes in exchange rates have a considerable impact on businesses in the UK. This is true even for those businesses that do not trade overseas. Small changes in the UK's exchange rate occur all the time because it is floating. A series of slight rises and falls over a period of time is not necessarily a major problem for industry. Of more concern is a sustained rise or fall in the exchange rate — or a sudden and substantial change.

Significant changes in the exchange rate can create a number of difficulties for businesses:

- Firms experience difficulty in forecasting earnings from overseas sales in the event of an exchange rate change taking place between agreeing the price (in the foreign currency) and receiving payment.
- Costs of imported raw materials can vary because of exchange rate fluctuations. A price quoted to customers might suddenly become unprofitable if the price paid for raw materials from overseas rises.
- Significant exchange rate fluctuations can change the price charged overseas for a product. A rise in the value of the pound makes it more difficult for exporters, while a fall in the value of the pound can help exporters to be more price competitive.

It is important to be able to analyse the effects of a change in the value of the pound on a business. Table 7.5 summarises these changes.

exchange rate — the price of one currency expressed in terms of another

Examiner's tip

When discussing prices (in connection with exchange rates), don't ignore price elasticity. For example, if overseas demand for a product is price inelastic, an increase in the exchange rate may not be harmful.

Table 7.5 Effects on a business of a change in the value of the pound

Exchange value of the pound	Prices of UK exports overseas in local currency	Prices of products imported into the UK in pounds sterling
Increases (appreciates)	Rise	Fall
Decreases (depreciates)	Fall	Rise

Changes in exchange rates only affect the price at which imports and exports are sold. Exchange rates are an important issue for businesses selling in price-competitive international markets. However, a number of other factors influence purchasing decisions in international markets:

- the reputation and quality of the product in question
- the design and functions of the product
- the after-sales service provided
- delivery dates and the business's record in meeting them

In some circumstances, a small change in the exchange rate can eliminate a firm's profit margin or make the firm uncompetitive.

Now test yourself

4 State in each of the following cases whether prices will rise or fall:
   (a) the price of exports if the exchange rate falls
   (b) the price of imports if the exchange rate rises
   (c) the price of exports if the exchange rate rises

Answers on p. 110

Tested

The globalisation of markets

Globalisation refers to the trend for many markets to become worldwide in scope. Because of globalisation, many businesses trade throughout the world, whereas in the past they may have focused on a single continent such as Europe. One reason why globalisation is so controversial is because different groups can interpret it in many different ways.

globalisation — the trend for many markets to become worldwide in scope

Fears about globalisation

For some groups, globalisation is a uniquely threatening word. It prompts visions of large multinationals dominating the world. Many groups fear that globalisation threatens the environment as well as national cultures, and predict that it will make the rich nations richer while impoverishing developing countries.

Citizens in rich and poor countries alike see the threat posed to their local cultures by globalisation, and have acted to protect them. Throughout the world, people are battling to preserve their cultural identities against the forces of global commerce.

The benefits of globalisation

Of course, many governments and businesses have an entirely different view of globalisation. They believe that increased and freer trade between nations will offer prosperity and growth for all countries and businesses. Globalisation, they argue, has already brought many benefits: global food production has risen steadily over the last 20 years and malnutrition rates have fallen. Citizens in less developed countries have access to healthcare. For its supporters, globalisation offers an opportunity rather than posing a threat. The leaders of the world's major economies and big businesses are committed to protecting and promoting global commerce and trade, and reject claims of 'cultural imperialism' made against some large multinational companies.

> **Examiner's tip**
>
> When assessing the likely impact of globalisation, it helps to consider how this change will affect a range of the business's stakeholders. This will help you to make varied arguments and to make and support judgements.

Developments in emerging markets
Revised

The term **emerging markets** refers to those countries that are experiencing rapid industrialisation and the creation of a range of manufacturing industries. Examples of emerging markets include China, India, Mexico, Brazil, Argentina, Peru and a number of countries in eastern Europe.

> **emerging markets** — those countries that are experiencing rapid industrialisation and the creation of a range of manufacturing industries

Economies that are industrialising rapidly are likely to share a number of characteristics:

- rapid increases in the production of manufactured goods
- production of manufactured goods at lower prices
- a steady development of service industries
- an improved infrastructure as transport and communications are developed
- rising incomes for at least some of the population

Opportunities in emerging markets

Emerging markets offer a range of opportunities to businesses in developed countries such as the UK:

- They provide a source of cheap finished products. Many of the clothes sold by high-street retailers in the UK are made in Asia where labour costs are much lower.
- Increasingly, emerging markets provide attractive low-cost locations for UK-owned manufacturing businesses. As markets have become global, locating elsewhere in the world has fewer implications in terms of transport costs.

The threat posed by emerging nations

Emerging markets pose a competitive threat to businesses in the developed world. Low costs of production mean that they are able to be extremely price competitive. Over time, businesses in emerging nations have manufactured more sophisticated products and pose a major threat to established producers.

Demand from businesses in emerging markets has seen rising prices for raw materials such as oil, grain and industrial materials like lead and copper. This has increased the production costs of most businesses.

Response to changes in the economic environment
Revised

It is important to recognise that changes in the economic environment can offer opportunities as well as posing threats. A change such as the emergence of China as a major economy might offer both simultaneously. A business may consider a number of responses to economic change:

- **Rationalisation.** This entails reducing the scale of the business, possibly by closing down less profitable elements.
- **Capacity increase or reduction.** A change in the economic environment may alter demand for a firm's products. Firms may respond by reducing capacity (reducing employees' hours or mothballing factories) or by increasing capacity by subcontracting work to other businesses or creating new capacity.
- **Seeking new markets.** Economic change may make other markets more accessible, or more attractive, if the 'home' market suffers from adverse economic change.
- **Producing new products.** Rising incomes may mean that consumers have more money to spend on luxury items, including long-haul holidays in exotic locations.
- **Mergers and takeovers.** This could be an appropriate response to a variety of economic changes. Larger, more diverse businesses may be better suited to cope with the challenges of globalisation, or the problems of a major international economic downturn.

These are only a few possible responses to economic change. The exact responses will depend on the precise circumstances of the business and may vary enormously between businesses.

> **Now test yourself**
>
> 5 Explain the circumstances in which rationalisation might be an appropriate response to the threat posed by businesses in emerging markets.
>
> **Answers on p. 110**
>
> Tested

Business and the political and legal environment

This topic also requires you to evaluate strategies that businesses might deploy in response to changes in the political and legal environment.

Government intervention in the economy
Revised

Government provision of products

UK central and local governments provide a range of products. The government supplies some products because it is impractical for private organisations to do so, as in the case of defence. In other circumstances, products such as health and education are provided free of charge to the user to prevent the products being under-consumed.

Regulation of markets

Regulation means that the government intervenes in the operation of the market. For example, the government created Ofgem to promote competition and to control the monopoly companies that run the gas and electricity networks. Ofgem encourages gas and electricity suppliers to take environmentally friendly decisions and to look after the interests of vulnerable customers such as the disabled and elderly.

> **regulation** — government intervention in the operation of the market

Taxation and subsidy

In other cases, the government intervenes in the supply of products through taxation. Tobacco and alcohol are taxed in part to discourage consumption of these harmful products and in part to raise revenue for the government. In contrast, the government offers subsidies to encourage the production of green energy, such as electricity generated by wind farms.

Government economic policies

Revised

The government implements a series of policies designed to provide a stable and prosperous economic environment for businesses.

Fiscal policy

Fiscal policy refers to government policies based on taxation and its own expenditure.

> **Fiscal policy** — government policies based on taxation and its own expenditure

Taxation

The government can raise the level of economic activity in the UK by lowering the rates of taxation. The effects of such changes are outlined in Table 7.6.

Table 7.6 The effects of increases and reductions in taxation

The effects of increases in taxation	The effects of reductions in taxation
• Increases in indirect taxes such as VAT result in higher prices, cutting consumer demand.	• Cutting indirect taxes reduces prices, which may boost spending — especially for price-elastic products.
• Producers may pay the increase in indirect taxes to avoid raising prices; this will cut profits and may reduce investment levels by businesses.	• Reductions in income tax result in consumers having higher incomes. This increases demand, particularly for luxury products.
• Increases in income tax leave consumers with less disposable income, again reducing demand.	• Falling corporate taxation promotes investment and output by businesses, increasing economic activity.
	• Reductions in corporate taxation may attract investment by foreign individuals and businesses.

It is relatively easy to forecast the impact of changes in taxation rates on the overall level of economic activity. But the effects of these changes vary between individual firms. Businesses producing price-elastic goods will be affected by changes in indirect taxes, as demand is sensitive to price. Other firms may find their sales affected by alterations in the rates of direct taxation. Firms selling products such as foreign holidays or jewellery will be sensitive to changes in consumers' incomes; those selling basic foodstuffs are less likely to be affected.

Government expenditure

Government expenditure is the other part of fiscal policy. It can be placed into two categories:

● **Transfer payments.** This is government spending on pensions, unemployment benefit and similar social security payments. Alterations in this category of government expenditure have a rapid and significant impact on consumers' spending and the level of economic activity.

- **Spending on the nation's infrastructure.** Spending on such things as roads, schools and harbours can have a double impact on businesses. First, the results of the expenditure can enhance the environment for firms by improving communications and cutting the costs of transportation. Second, the construction can provide work and income for firms, so boosting their profitability. The government can also encourage investment by companies through offering investment grants and tax relief (see Table 7.7).

Table 7.7 Fiscal policy and levels of economic activity

	Falling level of economic activity	**Rising level of economic activity**
Caused by	Reduced government spending or increased taxation.	Increased government expenditure or lower rates of taxation.
Likely effects	Increased unemployment, declining spending and production.	Inflation may appear while unemployment falls as imports increase.
Impact on business	Falling sales and downward pressure on prices. Rising numbers of bankruptcies, especially among small firms. Increased levels of inventories.	Rising wages and possible skill shortages. Sales rise and possibility of increasing prices. Increasing costs of raw materials and components.

Monetary policy

Monetary policy centres on adjusting the amount of money in circulation and hence the level of spending and economic activity. The most used element of monetary policy is adjusting interest rates, although monetary policy also includes altering the amount of money circulating in the economy through quantitative easing.

> **monetary policy** — centres on adjusting the amount of money in circulation and hence the level of spending and economic activity

Rises in interest rates depress the level of economic activity and reductions promote an expansion of economic activity. A rise in the level of interest rates in the UK will reduce the level of economic activity for a number of reasons:

- Individuals and businesses will tend to save more, so reducing the level of expenditure and production.
- Consumers will postpone or abandon plans to purchase goods on credit, as interest charges have risen.
- Businesses will take decisions to reduce investment plans, as the cost of borrowing has risen and fewer projects will be viable.
- Firms may reduce inventory levels in an attempt to reduce their need to borrow to obtain working capital.
- There may be upward pressure on costs, as firms face higher charges to service their long-term debt. This may result in increases in retail prices.
- There will be an increase in the exchange value of the pound through the mechanism outlined earlier. This will increase the price of UK exports while reducing the price of imports.

The impact of rising interest rates will depend on the size of the change as well as the initial rate. A small increase at a relatively high level of rates will have little impact, while a larger increase from a low base rate will have a significant impact.

Supply-side policies

Supply-side policies are designed to promote greater and more efficient markets and production. They have gained credence over recent years and are intended to improve the working of the economy by improving the operation of free markets. The main elements of supply-side policies are:

> **Now test yourself**
>
> 6 Draw a diagram to illustrate the effects of a fall in interest rates on UK businesses.
>
> **Answers on p. 110**
>
> Tested ☐

- **Improving the quality of the labour force.** This can be done through increasing training to provide a more committed and skilled labour force.
- **Limiting the power of trade unions.** One reason for restricting the power of trade unions has been to make the labour market work more effectively and to avoid the excessive wage increases and small increases in productivity that may be the result of trade union power.
- **Reducing labour costs.** By making the labour market work effectively, the government hopes to allow wages to reflect local conditions.

> **supply-side policies** — designed to promote greater and more efficient markets and production

Political decisions affecting trade and markets

Revised ☐

Political decisions by governments can have significant impacts on businesses and their trading activities.

- **Freeing entry to markets.** Decisions such as the one by the UK government to allow other businesses to compete with Royal Mail in the delivery of letters have had significant implications. This has permitted the entry of new businesses such as Business Post and has offered consumers and other businesses choice.
- **Encouraging international trade.** Governments can work together to take decisions such as reducing or removing tariffs (taxes on imports), and thereby encouraging trade between different countries. The World Trade Organization exists to promote international trade.
- **Decisions to improve infrastructure.** A country's infrastructure is its transport networks and other communication systems. Governments often take decisions to invest in improving these aspects of a country's stock of capital. Some businesses benefit from undertaking profitable work to improve the infrastructure on behalf of the government. In the long term, other businesses benefit from being able to use the infrastructure and to trade more efficiently.

Impact of legislation relating to businesses

Revised ☐

The European Union and the UK government play a major role in determining the environment in which firms operate, by implementing a range of legislation that affects businesses. The key areas of legislation that affect business are:

- health and safety
- employment protection
- consumer protection
- environmental protection
- competition policy

Health and safety legislation

Health and safety legislation has been enacted to discourage dangerous practices by businesses and to protect the workforce. The legislation focuses on the prevention of accidents. The main Act in the UK is the Health and Safety at Work Act (1974).

The main provisions of the Health and Safety at Work Act are designed to 'ensure as far as is reasonably practical' the health and safety of all staff at work. The UK's health and safety legislation is continuously updated under the provisions of the Health and Safety at Work Act to take account of changes in working practices.

> **Examiner's tip**
>
> Don't spend long periods learning the content of the various laws. A broad appreciation of the nature and scope of the relevant legislation is all that is required. When answering questions, focus on the impact of the laws on businesses and their responses.

For example, in 2011 health and safety legislation was extended to cover businesses working on projects such as wind farms outside UK territorial waters.

Health and safety legislation is an important issue for firms operating in the primary and secondary sectors of the economy. For example, construction companies impose rigorous health and safety policies and monitor incidents very closely to avoid their repetition.

Employment protection

Employment protection falls into two categories: individual labour law and collective labour law.

Individual labour law

This category of legislation grants protection to individuals. An example of this type of legislation is law relating to discrimination. Discrimination on grounds of sex in employment and education is unlawful under the Sex Discrimination Acts (1975, 1986) as reinforced by the Employment Act (1989).

Collective labour law

This legislation relates to industrial relations and trade union activities. An example of a relevant piece of legislation is the Employment Protection (Consolidation) Act (1978). This covers a number of aspects of employment, such as contracts of employment and rules relating to dismissal.

Consumer protection

Consumer protection encompasses a series of Acts designed to safeguard consumers against unfair trading practices and dangerous products. This is managed by the Office of Fair Trading, which also looks after competition policy. Examples of relevant legislation include the Sale of Goods Act (1979). This Act requires that a seller must ensure that the goods sold are of merchantable quality — that is, they must be undamaged and unbroken, fit for the particular purpose and as described by the manufacturer.

Consumers have become more knowledgeable and discerning in their purchases. They often conduct research (aided by publications such as *Which?*) before making major purchases.

Environmental protection

The government has passed a series of Acts of Parliament designed to protect the environment. Two are particularly important:

- Environmental Protection Act (1990). This introduced the notion of integrated pollution control and requires businesses to minimise pollution as a whole.
- Environment Act (1995). This legislation established the Environment Agency with the brief of coordinating and overseeing environmental protection.

The government imposes fines on firms that breach legislation relating to the protection of the environment. These are intended to force firms to bear the full costs of their production, although environmental pressure groups and other critics believe that the sums are not sufficient to deter major businesses.

The government also attempts to encourage 'greener' methods of production through the provision of grants. For example, the government funding is also supporting the development of environmentally friendly offshore wind farms to generate 'clean' electricity.

Competition policy

Competition policy deals with monopolies, mergers and restrictive practices. A **monopoly** can be defined as 'a situation where there are no close substitutes for the goods that a firm produces'. The result of monopolies could be that:

- consumers are exploited through excessive prices
- consumers are offered a poor service
- some firms face unfair competition

Key organisations relating to this area of legislation are the Office of Fair Trading and the Competition Commission. These bodies ensure that firms with a large share of the market do not act against the public interest; proposed mergers are investigated, competition is encouraged and restrictive practices are discouraged.

> **Typical mistake**
>
> Don't simply argue that complying with environmental laws will increase a business's costs. Ensuring compliance with such laws can help a business to gain a reputation as a 'good' business and employer.

Changes in the political and legal environment — Revised

This book can only give you a few prompts to consider in regard to how businesses respond to changes in the political and legal environment. The precise responses of a business will depend on a number of factors, including the type and size of the business, its objectives, the nature and competitiveness of the market in which it trades and the extent to which the proposed or actual change will affect it.

Political and legal changes can offer opportunities as well as imposing constraints on the activities of businesses. Legislation relating to minimum wage or discrimination is likely to constrain the activities of firms. However, in contrast, new markets have been created for businesses supplying training in environmental management. Firms also offer to supply environmental control equipment to minimise the possibility of environmental harm during production. Equally, a market exists for testing equipment to monitor emissions or the toxicity of waste products.

> **Examiner's tip**
>
> In an examination, think about the precise nature of the business about which you are writing. The impact of changes in government policy or legislation will depend upon the type of business and the market in which it trades.

Business and the social environment

Nature of changes in the social environment — Revised

Important changes in the social environment have included:

- the desire among consumers to purchase environmentally friendly products
- increasing concern expressed about the treatment of farm animals and a greater number of consumers opting to become vegetarians

● a demand for firms to meet the needs of other stakeholder groups apart from shareholders

● the increasing number of single-person households and their different patterns of demand

A business's social responsibilities are the duties it has towards its stakeholders — employees, customers and society at large — as well as towards its shareholders (see Figure 7.2). Some firms willingly embrace these responsibilities, while others do not.

Figure 7.2 The stakeholders of a business

A business may accept its social responsibilities for two reasons:

● It has a genuine belief in the stakeholder concept, which recognises the needs of all parties with an interest in the organisation.

● It believes that it can derive some positive publicity from being seen to be socially responsible.

Increasingly, firms are being asked to consider and justify their actions towards all stakeholders rather than just their shareholders. A number of issues arise as a result of these pressures:

● Even firms that have a genuine desire to change may experience difficulties in altering their existing culture.

● Meeting stakeholders' needs can lead to many benefits. These include: keeping existing customers and winning new ones; recruiting and keeping high-quality employees; and developing a positive long-term corporate image.

● The precise social responsibilities that a firm should meet vary from business to business and change over time.

It is unlikely that a business will be able to meet the needs of all interest groups. It is normal for some sort of trade-off to take place. By fulfilling the needs of one stakeholder group, the demands of others may be ignored. In a time of slump, when profits are reduced, businesses may be more likely to focus on meeting the needs of shareholders. In more prosperous periods, a broader range of stakeholders may be satisfied.

Social responsibilities are particularly important for some types of business. For example, firms producing relatively undifferentiated products may meet social responsibilities as fully as possible to provide a unique selling proposition.

Now test yourself

7 State one objective that each of following stakeholder groups might have from its association with a business that manufactures chemicals: shareholders, managers, employees, suppliers, the government and local residents.

Answers on p. 110

Tested ☐

Demographic changes

The population in the UK is changing in a number of ways. It is growing rapidly and is forecast to reach 65 million by 2031. At the same time, the population is becoming older: by 2040, 15 million people in the UK will be aged over 65. Simultaneously, the number of one-person households is increasing quickly: the figure has increased by more than 25% since 1991. Finally, the UK has become increasingly multicultural as a result of migration patterns over the last 50 years.

Environmental issues

Businesses face a number of issues in relation to the environment, including global warming, air and water pollution, and increasing expectations that they will recycle and use sustainable resources.

Environmental issues are important for manufacturing businesses and especially those with considerable potential to pollute the atmosphere. This is particularly true if the business sells directly to the public. Companies such as Shell and BP Amoco fall into this category and have to be especially careful about their public image with regard to environmental issues.

A 'balance sheet' of the potential costs and benefits for firms in acting in an environmentally responsible way is given in Table 7.8.

Now test yourself

8 Why might a large public limited company ignore its social responsibilities?

Answers on p. 110

Tested

Table 7.8 Environmental balance sheet

Potential benefits	Potential costs
• Firms may find it easier to raise funds if they have a good environmental record. For example, the Co-operative Bank will not lend money to businesses that damage the environment.	• Meeting strict environmental controls imposes additional costs on businesses, as they need to introduce new processes, retrain employees and use more expensive resources.
• Working for a business that genuinely cares about the environment can motivate employees and make it easier to recruit high-calibre staff.	• For a business to be sincere in protecting the environment, it is important for all employees to pursue this objective — it is not always easy to change the culture of a business.
• There are significant marketing advantages to be gained from adopting an environmentally friendly stance. The publicity given to environmental audits by many companies reflects this factor.	• Proper disposal of harmful by-products from manufacturing can be very expensive and may reduce profits to the dismay of shareholders.

The changing nature of the ethical environment

Revised

Ethics can be defined as a code of behaviour considered morally correct. Taking an ethical decision means doing what is morally right. It is not simply taking the decision that leads to the highest profits. Many activities in the business world have an ethical dimension: for example, should a manufacturing business use a cheap, non-sustainable source of timber or a more expensive, sustainable supply that would mean lower profits for shareholders?

To use non-sustainable sources of supply is not illegal, but many people would regard it as morally wrong (see Figure 7.3). Whether a business would turn down profitable (or cost-saving) opportunities such as these is debatable.

ethics — a code of behaviour considered morally correct

Figure 7.3 The law and ethical behaviour by businesses

The law protects society from the worst excesses of business behaviour. Thus, competition legislation prevents monopolies abusing their power, and employment protection legislation looks after the welfare of workers. Ethical behaviour requires businesses to take this process a step further. However, ethical behaviour offers benefits to business as well as imposing additional costs, as shown in Table 7.9.

Now test yourself

9 Give two examples of ethical decisions that businesses may take.

Answers on p. 110

Tested

Table 7.9 Advantages and disadvantages of ethical behaviour

Advantages	Disadvantages
• There are obvious benefits to a business that is perceived by the public as ethically correct. This may result in increased sales.	• Taking ethical decisions can be expensive. It may involve turning down highly profitable trading opportunities in favour of taking moral decisions.
• Having a positive ethical stance may assist a business in recruiting high-quality employees. It may also result in a lower turnover of staff.	• There may be conflict with existing staff or existing policies. For example, a policy of delegation may pose problems when attempting to promote a more ethical culture.

Behaving ethically in business

Ethically correct behaviour is not always easy to implement throughout an organisation for the following reasons:

● Senior managers may decide to adopt an ethical stance, but persuading other employees to follow their lead can be difficult.

● Firms that practise empowerment and delegation can experience problems in creating an ethical culture, as decision making is in the hands of a large number of employees. A potential conflict exists between ethical behaviour and delegation if budgets are delegated.

● Shareholders might be dissatisfied if dividends fall as a result of the company taking ethical decisions.

● What one person considers morally correct may be abhorred by others.

Typical mistake

Too many students assume that it is easy for a business to adopt ethical policies. This is not the case and it can take considerable time and resources to effect such a change in culture.

Actions to promote ethical behaviour

Businesses can take the following actions to promote ethical behaviour:

● **Training.** Businesses cannot expect employees automatically to operate within strict moral guidelines. Training is essential to prepare employees to act ethically.

● **Consistency.** Businesses need to develop an ethical code of practice to which employees will be expected to adhere.

Is ethical behaviour genuine?

Some businesses adopt an ethical stance for genuine reasons. The beliefs of senior managers may have shaped this policy and helped to give conviction to the stance. While the move may have proved profitable, it is possible in these cases to argue that morals have nevertheless been put before profits.

Other companies may have adopted an apparently ethical stance to improve the public's perception of the business and, ultimately, its profits. To adopt an ethical stance for public relations reasons is a dangerous policy. It may result in the policy being exposed by the media as a sham, with consequent damage to the business's corporate image.

Examiner's tip

There is obvious potential for setting evaluative questions in this area. There are clear commercial advantages resulting from adopting an ethical stance, principally in the field of marketing. At the same time, a business is likely to incur additional costs and possible internal conflict.

Corporate social responsibility Revised

Corporate social responsibility (CSR) is a concept whereby organisations consider the interests of society by taking responsibility for the impact of their activities on customers, suppliers, employees, shareholders, communities and other stakeholders, as well as the environment. This extends beyond a business's legal obligations and entails voluntarily taking steps to improve the quality of life for employees and for the local community and society at large.

CSR has been much criticised. Supporters put the business case for CSR, arguing that businesses benefit in multiple ways by operating with a perspective beyond short-term profits. Critics argue that CSR distracts from the fundamental economic role of businesses to make profits and keep shareholders content. Some people believe that CSR is only superficial window dressing.

As part of CSR, businesses use social and environmental audits to set objectives, to measure and to publicise the extent to which they operate in the interests of society at large.

> **corporate social responsibility (CSR)** — a concept whereby organisations consider the interests of society by taking responsibility for the impact of their activities on customers, suppliers, employees, shareholders, communities and other stakeholders, as well as the environment

Social audits

A **social audit** is an independent investigation into a firm's activities and their impact on society. Social audits cover pollution, waste and recycling materials. A social audit may be for internal consumption to assist managers in implementing socially responsible policies. Alternatively, or additionally, it may be used externally to project the image of a caring and responsible organisation, in the hope of attracting additional sales.

> **social audit** — an independent investigation into a firm's activities and their impact on society

Social audits provide some indication of the efficiency of a business that cannot be expressed in financial terms. They may provide information on the amount of recycling undertaken by the business and security of employment offered to the local community.

Environmental audits

Many businesses, including Shell, BP and The Body Shop, are conducting environmental audits to measure the impact of their operations on the environment. These are similar in nature to social audits but focus specifically on issues such as pollution and waste disposal. These audits can provide useful data for managers in their decision making, as well as contributing positively to a business's corporate image.

> **Now test yourself**
>
> 10 Why might many firms not use social audits?
>
> Answers on p. 111
>
> Tested

Business and the technological environment

Effects of technological change Revised

Technology is advancing at an ever-increasing rate and affects both processes and products. Technological developments include the development of more advanced and sophisticated computers and the use of nanotechnology in a range of products.

Technological advances have created new products and new ways of producing products. But advances in technology mean that computers can be sold in different ways. One of the world's leading manufacturers, Dell, sells its products via the internet rather than through high street retailers. This keeps costs to a minimum, boosting profitability.

Developments in technology have dramatically improved the process of production for many firms — services as well as manufacturing. The development of computer-aided design has made new products easier to design, store and alter. Modern software can also be used to estimate the cost of newly designed products. Technology has revolutionised manufacturing too. Computer-aided manufacturing is used by manufacturing firms of all sizes.

Benefits of new technology

New technology offers businesses and consumers a range of benefits:

- Reduced unit costs of production, enhancing the competitiveness of the business concerned. For example, Boeing, the US aircraft manufacturer, designs much of its new aircraft on computers and can assemble 'virtual aircraft'. This reduces the company's use of expensive prototypes.
- In the case of high-technology products, such as new games consoles, the opportunity to charge a premium price until the competition catches up. Such price skimming is likely to boost profits.

Costs of new technology

New technology also poses difficulties for many businesses. For example:

- It is likely to be a drain on an organisation's capital. In some circumstances, firms may experience difficulty in raising the funds necessary to install high-technology equipment.
- It inevitably requires training of the existing workforce and perhaps recruitment of new employees. Both actions can create considerable costs for businesses.
- Its introduction may be met with opposition from existing employees, especially if job security is threatened. This may lead to industrial action.

> **Examiner's tip**
>
> Consider the impact of changes in the technological environment in both the short term and the long term. It may be the case that the major benefits do not accrue in the short term.

Response to changes in the technological environment

Revised ☐

Developing new products

Some businesses have based their corporate strategies on the development of new technology. Apple is well known for its innovative products, even though it does not commit huge sums of money to research and development. Other businesses, such as Microsoft, deploy the same corporate strategy, embracing technological change and using it as the key element in selling its products. In this way, these companies use technological change to enhance their products.

Exam practice answers and quick quizzes at **www.therevisionbutton.co.uk/myrevisionnotes**

Adopting new processes

Technology offers businesses the opportunity to improve the efficiency of their operations process. Thus rapid advances in communications technology have allowed UK banks to set up call centres in India where wage costs are much lower than in the UK. Technology has also been used extensively by manufacturers to improve the performance of their businesses. The use of virtual aircraft design by Boeing means that it can make sure the various parts will fit and operate together. Changes and alterations can be made before any element of the product is actually manufactured.

Using traditional approaches to develop a USP

Some businesses deliberately avoid the technological approach to production or to the resulting products. For example, the traditional wooden toy market has survived despite fierce competition from products incorporating the latest technology. Some banks advertise that they have a bank manager whom you can meet and speak with. Their stance is that you will not always be dealing with technology. Banks using this approach hope to gain a competitive advantage.

> **Now test yourself**
>
> 11 Identify two businesses in which developing a non-technological traditional approach as a USP may be a feasible strategy.
>
> **Answers on p. 111**
>
> Tested ☐

Business and the competitive environment

Changes in the competitive structure of markets
Revised ☐

Arrival of new competitors

The arrival of new competitors can have a number of effects on a market:

- **Driving prices down.** It can encourage existing businesses to offer more competitive prices or to develop strategies to differentiate themselves from the new businesses. This may benefit consumers but could also lead to diminished quality if profit margins are slim.

- **New products offering customers additional choices and possibly extending the market.** The G-Wiz electric car has been designed for city driving and to be environmentally friendly. The car was designed in California and is manufactured by the Indo-US Reva Electric Car Company. It may have resulted in fewer sales for existing car manufacturers, but may also have developed a new niche market in which existing producers may compete. So, a new competitor can stimulate a market.

- **The closure of some existing producers.** The least efficient producers in the market may not survive the entry of new, more competitive businesses. This can reduce consumer choice and may result in a few large businesses dominating a market.

> **Examiner's tip**
>
> This is an obvious area for considering the different opinions of stakeholders. Such an approach may help you to develop evaluation.

Creation of dominant businesses

Firms can become dominant in markets through **mergers** (joining with other businesses) or through **takeovers** (when one business purchases control of another). The resulting business will be larger and will have greater influence in the market. It will be more able to influence market prices, to exercise control over supplies of materials and components, or to invest in research and development to create new products and processes.

Changes in the buying power of customers

As some businesses increase in scale, they can become the largest or even sole customers of other businesses. It is not uncommon for supermarkets in the UK to be the sole customers of farmers or other food producers. This gives the supermarkets a powerful hand in negotiating prices and contract terms. Possessing considerable buying power can be a major advantage to a business if it is selling its products in a price-competitive market.

Changes in the selling power of suppliers

If a supplier has a dominant position in a market, it has greater freedom to choose prices and general conditions of sale. This situation applies in the global energy market, where the Russian government has substantial control over the sale of oil and gas to businesses in western Europe. Suppliers with selling power may only be able to exercise such power in the short term, especially if they exploit it to charge what customers consider to be excessive prices. The reaction of customers in this situation will be to find alternative suppliers.

Response to changes in the competitive environment

Revised

Businesses can respond in a variety of ways to changes in the competitive environment. Their responses will depend on the precise circumstances.

- **Takeovers or mergers.** A move towards a more oligopolistic market structure may result in smaller firms in that market joining together or buying one another, to give the new business sufficient scale to compete with larger rivals.

- **Producing new products or cutting prices.** The arrival of new competitors or the creation of a dominant business may lead to existing producers increasing the range of products they offer or engaging in price cutting.

- **Seeking new markets.** Existing businesses could respond to new competitors or to dominant businesses by seeking to develop new markets where competition is less fierce. Some business airlines have moved to new routes when faced with direct competition from budget airlines.

- **Developing a different corporate strategy.** Increasing competition may lead to a business adopting a different strategy, such as becoming more innovative or moving to supply a different segment of the market — perhaps consumers seeking more exclusive products.

Examiner's tip

When responding to questions about changes in the competitive environment, you should consider the circumstances carefully. In developing your response, consider the strengths and weaknesses of the business, the resources available to it and the timescale over which it is able to respond.

Check your understanding

Tested

1   Define the phrase 'the level of economic activity'.
2   What is meant by the term 'ethics'?
3   Define the term 'social audit'.
4   Explain how a rise in unemployment might affect a major retailer in the UK.
5   Define the term 'exchange rate'.
6   Outline the implications of a fall in the exchange rate for a business that imports raw materials and exports finished products.
7   Define the term 'globalisation'.
8   Outline two opportunities that may be created for UK businesses in emerging markets.
9   Explain the difference between fiscal policy and monetary policy.
10 Explain why a rise in the level of interest rates will reduce the level of economic activity.
11 Why might the existence of health and safety legislation improve the performance of a business's workforce?
12 Explain why a business might opt to take ethical decisions.
13 Outline the factors that may increase the degree of competitiveness in a market.
14 Is an increase in economic activity always good for businesses?
15 Explain how technological advances may cause problems for businesses.

Answers on p. 111

Exam practice

Essays

1   The UK economy has performed relatively poorly since the recession of 2008, with low levels of economic growth and dampened levels of economic activity. Do you think that this will inevitably have damaged the profits of UK businesses? Justify your answer with reference to businesses with which you are familiar.   [40]

2   The US multinational companies Apple and Amazon have responded to technological change by producing new products incorporating the latest technology. Do you think this is the best way for businesses to respond to changes in technology? Justify your answer with reference to Apple, Amazon and/or other businesses with which you are familiar.   [40]

Answers and quick quiz online

Online

8 Managing change

Internal causes of change

Changes in an organisation's size Revised

There are a number of reasons why an organisation might change its scale and thereby generate change within the organisation.

Mergers and takeovers

A **merger** is the combining of two or more firms into a single business following agreement by the firms' management teams and shareholders. A **takeover** occurs when one company acquires complete control of another by purchasing over 50% of its share capital. The types of merger and takeover are shown in Table 8.1.

> **merger** — the combining of two or more firms into a single business following agreement by the firms' management teams and shareholders
>
> **takeover** — when one company acquires complete control of another by purchasing over 50% of its share capital

Table 8.1 Types of merger and takeover

Mergers	Takeovers
Mergers may be: <ul><li>Horizontal — between firms at the same stage of production in the same market, offering economies of scale.</li><li>Vertical — between firms operating at different levels in the same market, providing certainty of supply or retail outlets.</li><li>Conglomerate — between firms in unrelated markets, reducing risk and allowing the transfer of good practice.</li></ul>	Takeovers may be horizontal, vertical or conglomerate. They can also be: <ul><li>Hostile — where a predator company's attentions are unwelcome and the target may try to reject the move. The predator has only a limited time to persuade the target company's shareholders to accept the bid.</li><li>Friendly — where the company to be taken over welcomes the purchase and is likely to recommend that shareholders accept the bid.</li></ul>

The growing competitive pressure in a number of UK markets has forced many companies to merge in an attempt to increase efficiency by operating on a larger scale.

Businesses engage in mergers and takeovers for a number of reasons:

- **Growth.** Mergers and takeovers can be easy methods of expansion. However, it can be risky to spend large sums of capital on combining with another, perhaps relatively unknown, business.

- **Managers can often derive satisfaction and career enhancement** from increasing the scale of their organisation.

- A business may merge with or take over another company to achieve the benefits of **economies of scale**. This is most likely with horizontal mergers.

- Mergers and takeovers may be undertaken to **protect market share**, by purchasing a rival that may prove a threat in years to come.

Sometimes **demergers** follow a takeover that has not been successful, perhaps because the expected economies of scale have not materialised.

Alternatively, companies may decide to sell off peripheral divisions to concentrate on their core activities.

Organic growth

Organic growth is a process of business expansion resulting from increased production, sales or both, rather than mergers or takeovers. It is a good indicator of how well the business's management has used its resources to expand the organisation's profits.

Organic growth can be created in a number of ways, such as:

- successful promotion of the business's products
- maximising value added
- introducing innovative products

A business may need to borrow heavily to finance organic growth, although some businesses such as McDonald's achieve this through the use of franchising.

Retrenchment

Retrenchment occurs when a business becomes smaller. In effect, this is negative organic growth. There are a number of possible causes of retrenchment:

- changes in tastes and fashions
- technological developments making products obsolete
- the closure of subsidiary businesses

Now test yourself

1 Draw a table to show the likely impact of mergers and takeovers on a business's major stakeholder groups.

Answers on p. 111

Tested

organic growth — a process of business expansion resulting from increased production, sales or both, rather than mergers or takeovers

retrenchment — occurs when a business becomes smaller. In effect, this is negative organic growth

Examiner's tip

In the case of each of these causes of change, you should think about the effects on the organisation. Key issues might include levels of employment, product range and corporate image.

How new owners or leaders can cause change

Revised

It is not unusual for a business to have new owners and this can be a spur to change. For example, a business might be taken over by another, larger organisation, or one business might sell a subsidiary company.

The consequences of a new owner will depend to some extent on why the business has changed ownership. If the new owner was seeking an established and valued brand, the extent of change resulting might be relatively slight. The new owner would want to maintain the image and product range. However, a new owner might have purchased a business because of the possibilities of improving its performance and generating higher profits. This could lead to substantial changes within the business, including job loss or entry into new markets.

Poor business performance as a catalyst for change

Revised

A business may perform badly by allowing its product range to become outdated. However, the performance of most private sector businesses is judged most effectively by financial measures. Thus, a business suffering from declining profits or a substantial reduction in its share price may be purchased by another business.

A decline in profitability is often the catalyst for change in companies. Shareholders will be unhappy in such circumstances, as their dividends may be cut, or no dividends may be paid. This can be accompanied by

Now test yourself

2 Compile a list of the factors that might constitute poor performance for a business.

Answers on p. 111

Tested

falling share prices, resulting in capital losses. This is likely to provoke calls for change, and directors may be voted out of office by angry shareholders.

The other key cause of poor business performance which acts as a catalyst for change is a lack of cash flow. If a severe shortage of cash occurs, a company become insolvent, in which case it is legally obliged to cease trading. In such a situation, a business is vulnerable to takeover. In any event, a shortage of cash often results in dramatic changes within an organisation.

Planning for change

The purpose of corporate plans
Revised

Corporate plans

A **corporate (or strategic) plan** is a long-term strategy by which a business hopes to achieve its corporate objectives. This type of planning involves matching the corporate objectives to the resources available. The corporate plan is therefore the strategic process of allocating resources within an organisation in order to achieve its strategic or corporate aims.

> **corporate (or strategic) plan** — a long-term strategy by which a business hopes to achieve its corporate objectives

The purpose of corporate plans is to make sure that managers are looking ahead and thinking about what they want to achieve and how to achieve it, rather than just drifting along. Producing the plan is also a useful exercise because it forces managers to consider the organisation's strengths and weaknesses in relation to its environment, and to think about how all the different elements of the firm interrelate.

Corporate plans also have an important function of ensuring that the separate departments (marketing, finance, HR and operations) are working together in pursuit of the business's overall or corporate objectives. The corporate plan pulls together the functional plans and provides a sense of common purpose.

Contingency planning

All plans, and especially long-term ones, can go wrong. Businesses should prepare for this and also for the unexpected. A business may put a contingency plan into operation in the following circumstances:

- **During a sudden slump in demand.** This can result in extreme difficulties if revenues drop suddenly and unexpectedly.
- **When a business becomes the object of the attentions of a pressure group.** Attracting a great deal of adverse publicity can lead to managers planning a major change of strategy.
- **When a new and highly efficient competitor emerges.** For example, British Airways sales have suffered as a result of the emergence of easyJet and Ryanair as rivals.

> **Typical mistake**
>
> Don't confuse corporate and contingency plans, but do remember to consider both if the question simply refers to 'planning'.

Contingency plans should contain a number of common elements:

- an identified team headed by an experienced manager to assume control in the event of a crisis

- sufficient financial, human and technological resources to deal with the problem
- effective communications systems that can identify the nature and causes of the problem as well as prepare appropriate responses
- efficient links with the media, as ill-informed speculation can be damaging to the organisation

Contingency plans need to be reviewed regularly to ensure that they are relevant and up to date. It may be necessary to test the effectiveness of contingency plans and systems by simulating a crisis and practising the planned response.

Influences on corporate plans — Revised

A number of internal and external factors may influence senior managers in constructing their corporate or strategic plans.

Internal factors

- **The organisation's mission statement and corporate objectives.** If, for example, these make reference to becoming market leader, the associated corporate plan will probably address issues such as quality, customer service and takeovers.
- **The resources available to the business.** Grand plans for expansion may founder if a business has access to only relatively small amounts of finance. Similarly, improving customer service may require greater and more skilled human resources than those available to the business. Strategies are normally based on a business's strengths.

External factors

Factors outside the organisation are likely to have a substantial impact on the contents of its corporate plan.

- **The actions of competitors.** Managers set corporate objectives and plan their associated strategies to achieve these objectives with the aim of operating in profitable markets. Actions of competitors (e.g. a competitor bringing out a new and revolutionary product) can affect the profitability of markets and corporate objectives.
- **The state of the market and the economy.** A growing market is likely to result in more expansive corporate plans, not least because the business will probably have access to greater quantities of resources, including funding. A recession will result in more conservative corporate plans.

It is normal for corporate plans to be determined and operated by senior managers within the business. However, some business analysts, such as Tom Peters, have argued that autonomous workgroups should contribute to the generation of corporate plans. Over recent years, large companies, such as British Airways, have introduced staff training with the aim of reinforcing company values and encouraging all staff to contribute to the achievement of corporate objectives.

> **Examiner's tip**
>
> The specification requires you to evaluate the importance of influences on corporate plans such as those set out here. You should be prepared to make and justify judgements about the most important influences on a business's corporate plans. Think about whether external or internal influences are more dominant and make sure that you understand the company's financial position and its market standing.

A corporate plan offers two major advantages to a business. First, the process of corporate planning requires senior managers in an organisation to look forward and to consider where they want the organisation to be and how it should achieve these objectives. This process can encourage managers to consider the strengths and weaknesses of the business and how these can be used to respond to threats and to take advantage of any opportunities that may exist. This process should help to develop a more proactive style of management, assisting businesses to become innovative and market leaders.

The second benefit is coordination. In large businesses, possibly trading in many markets across several countries, a corporate plan can guide all managers in drawing up their plans. Thus, the sometimes disparate elements of the organisation can work together to achieve common goals.

But there are dangers in slavishly following a corporate plan, especially in a changing environment. It can result in managers taking incorrect decisions. An effective corporate plan should be a work in progress.

> **Now test yourself**
>
> 3 Draw a diagram to illustrate the circumstances in which corporate planning is particularly important.
>
> **Answers on p. 111**
>
> Tested

Leadership and the change process

The meaning of leadership

A **leader** is a person who rules, guides or inspires others. Leaders have authority that has been delegated to them by the organisation.

A good leader has a number of qualities, which may include:

- being informed and knowledgeable
- having the ability to think creatively and innovatively
- having the ability to act decisively
- possessing an air of authority
- having first-class communication skills (including listening)
- being able to solve problems, often under pressure

> **Leader** — a person who rules, guides or inspires others

A leader differs from a manager. A manager sets objectives and seeks the most efficient use of resources. A leader motivates people and brings the best out of individuals in pursuit of agreed objectives.

The range of leadership styles

Some writers on leadership have argued that leaders are born. This is known as **trait theory**. Such analysts attempt to identify the features of personality that one would expect to find in a good leader, as in the list above. Others have rejected this view and contend that people can be taught to be good leaders. This school of thought gives a central role to **training** in successful leadership.

In spite of the above dispute, four basic categories of leadership style are used widely for purposes of analysis. These are **democratic**, **paternalistic**, **authoritarian** and **laissez-faire**. Each style has advantages and disadvantages, and each is perhaps appropriate in particular circumstances (see Table 8.2).

Table 8.2 Leadership styles

	Democratic	Paternalistic	Authoritarian	Laissez-faire
Description	Democratic leadership entails running a business on the basis of decisions agreed by the majority.	The paternalistic approach is dictatorial, but decisions are intended to be in the best interests of the employees.	An authoritarian leadership style keeps information and decision making among the senior managers.	Laissez-faire leadership means the leader has a peripheral role, leaving staff to manage the business.
Key features	Encourages participation and makes use of delegation.	Leader explains decisions and ensures social and leisure needs are met.	Sets objectives and allocates tasks. Leader retains control throughout.	Leader evades duties of management and uncoordinated delegation occurs.
Communication	Extensive, two-way. Encourages contributions from subordinates.	Generally downwards, though feedback will take place.	One-way communication, downwards from leader to subordinates.	Mainly horizontal communication, though little communication occurs.
Uses	When complex decisions are made requiring a range of specialist skills.	Can appear democratic, but is really 'soft' autocracy.	Useful when quick decisions are required.	Can encourage production of highly creative work by subordinates.
Advantages	Commitment to business, satisfaction and quality of work may all improve.	Can engender loyalty, and frequently enjoys low labour turnover due to emphasis on social needs.	Decisions and direction of business will be consistent. May project image of confident, well-managed business.	May bring the best out of highly professional or creative groups.
Disadvantages	Slow decision making and need for consensus may avoid taking 'best' decisions.	Really autocratic and can result in groups becoming highly dependent. They may become dissatisfied with leader.	Lack of information, so subordinates are highly dependent on leaders; supervision needed.	May not be deliberate, but bad management — staff lack focus and sense of direction. Much dissatisfaction.

Influences on leadership styles

Revised

Leadership styles may vary according to the circumstances. The appropriate method will depend on the personality of the leader, the ability and skills of the workforce and the timescale. There are also a number of internal and external factors which may influence the leadership style adopted.

● **The culture of the business.** If employees are used to autocratic management, preparation and (especially) training will be required before a change of style.

● **The nature of the task.** For example, a complex and lengthy task is more likely to need democratic management.

● **The nature of the workforce.** Less skilled and large groups of employees might be more likely to respond to autocratic styles of management. The personalities and potential of the workforce will also influence the style of leadership adopted.

- **The personality and skills of the leader.** Good communication and other interpersonal skills might encourage democratic leadership. Alternatively, high levels of knowledge of the task may encourage a more autocratic approach.

- **Takeovers and mergers.** If a business is taken over by or merges with another organisation, the leadership style may change to reflect the changed ownership of the organisation. A business taking over another may impose its own management team and leadership style.

Tannenbaum and Schmidt developed this idea further. They argued that the style of leadership depends on the prevailing circumstances. Leaders should have the ability to exercise a range of leadership styles and should deploy them as appropriate. Therefore, a good leader is one who has the talent to adapt his or her style to the circumstances. Table 8.3 illustrates the range or continuum of styles a leader might use.

Examiner's tip

Leadership styles link to many other factors within a business, including HR strategies, corporate culture and corporate objectives. Analysing such links can provide important lines of argument when responding to essays or research questions.

Table 8.3 Tannenbaum and Schmidt's continuum of leadership behaviour

Use of authority by the leader				Degree of freedom enjoyed by subordinates	
Tells	**Sells**	**Tests**	**Consults**	**Joins**	**Delegates**
Leader	*Leader*	*Leader*	*Leader*	*Leader*	*Leader*
Owns and resolves total problem and instructs subordinates.	Resolves problem and informs subordinates.	Tackles problem but seeks opinions.	Proposes alternatives and seeks recommendations.	Works with subordinates in taking decisions.	Passes authority to subordinates for decision making.
Subordinate	*Subordinate*	*Subordinate*	*Subordinate*	*Subordinate*	*Subordinate*
Simply responds.	Receives explanation and acts.	Expresses views on decision.	Discusses alternatives and gives recommendations.	Helps shape objectives and solutions. Views accepted.	Exercises authority and owns the decisions taken.

The role of leadership in managing change

Revised ☐

Leadership can influence the process of change profoundly in a number of ways:

- **Setting objectives.** Leaders establish the goals that the change process is intended to achieve. By setting realistic, appropriate but challenging goals, the leader can set the tone of the entire process and provide it with a sense of purpose and direction.

- **Appointing or being the change project 'champion'.** We will consider this more fully on p. 104, but the leader can be a role model for change and support its cause at every opportunity.

- **Making sufficient resources available at the right time.** A leader will have ultimate control of financial, human and other resources, and by making them available at the right time, he or she can lubricate the wheels of change. For example, a business planning to extend its product range may need large sums of finance at an early stage in the process to pay staff salaries and for research and development.

- **Using available talent as fully as possible.** Change can be a pressured and stressful time for an organisation. A good leader will seek to make use of all the talents that are available within the organisation to manage it as effectively as possible. The leader may also recognise the need to bring in external expertise to manage change.

The importance of leadership

Revised

Does it really matter to a business whether it has highly skilled and conscientious leaders? As in so many cases, the answer to this will depend on the circumstances, as shown in Table 8.4.

In spite of this distinction, it is probably true to say that good leadership is important in the long term for any business. Even a business with a strong market share, high profits and well-established brands may find its position declining unless appropriate decisions and actions are taken. Rivals may develop new, more sophisticated products that are highly valued by consumers. Sales and profits may diminish and the firm's position in the market may decline. A business (or a leader) should not take success for granted.

Table 8.4 The importance of leadership

When good leadership would be really important	When good leadership may be desirable, but not so critical
• In a highly competitive market, where profit margins are slim. • In the early stages of a business's life, when it is attempting to establish itself. • At a time of particularly rapid and substantial change. • At a time of crisis — for example, when consumers lose confidence in a product, or a takeover is threatened.	• When a business is well established with strong brands and high levels of consumer loyalty. • In a market where patterns of demand change infrequently. • Where the workforce is highly skilled and motivated — the role of a leader might be more administrative in these circumstances.

Culture and the change process

Types of organisational culture

Revised

An organisation's **culture** is the attitudes, ideas and beliefs that are shared by its employees. An organisation's culture develops over time in response to many factors.

Various different types of organisational culture exist. The list below is based on the writing of Charles Handy.

- **Traditional or role culture.** Businesses with this type of culture are conventional, operate in a bureaucratic manner and value conventional behaviour. Employees are expected to follow the rules and emphasis is given to hierarchy and roles within the organisation.

- **Person-orientated culture.** This focuses on fulfilling the needs of individuals within an organisation. It allows individuals freedom to shape their jobs and operate with a degree of independence.
- **Task culture.** This focuses on solving problems. Expert teams or groups are assembled to tackle particular problems or to complete projects. This culture attaches importance to expertise, flexibility and creativity.
- **Power culture.** This places considerable emphasis on personal charisma and risk taking. It disregards procedures and values entrepreneurship.

In addition, a **change culture** can be highly valued in some circumstances. This refers to a flexible, responsive organisation that is capable of adapting effectively and quickly to external stimuli.

> **culture** — the attitudes, ideas and beliefs that are shared by an organisation's employees

> **Now test yourself**
>
> 4 Make a list of the factors that might assist a business in changing its culture successfully.
>
> **Answers on p. 111–112**
>
> Tested

Changing organisational culture

Revised

Reasons for changing culture

Changing corporate cultures has attracted a great deal of attention in management circles over recent years. Some managers consider that their organisations have an inappropriate culture. For example, a business with a role culture, with closely defined and highly specialised jobs, may find it difficult to operate in a fiercely competitive market that requires adaptability and a high degree of creativity from employees.

An organisation may seek to change its culture for a number of other reasons:

- It may be subject to a takeover bid or have agreed a merger with another business, and the organisation's existing culture conflicts with that of the other organisation.
- Changing locations may result in cultures being considered inappropriate. For example, a business relocating much of its operation overseas may consider that a traditional culture is less effective when people are in several distant locations. It may be that the business seeks to move towards a task culture in these circumstances.
- The appointment of a new chief executive may be the catalyst for changing a culture. If this is an external appointment and the new employee has been highly successful in an organisation with a different culture, he or she may decide to introduce the same culture.
- Managers may consider that the present culture makes the business uncompetitive. For example, if rivals are more flexible and responsive to changing market conditions, the managers of a business may seek to move from a traditional to a task-orientated culture.

Problems in changing culture

If a culture is strongly embedded within the organisation, it may prove difficult to change. A number of factors determine how strong an organisation's culture may be:

Exam practice answers and quick quizzes at **www.therevisionbutton.co.uk/myrevisionnotes**

- **The rate of labour turnover.** If a business experiences a low level of labour turnover, the prevailing culture is likely to be reinforced. Change is easier to effect when a large number of new employees enter the business regularly.

- **The nature and background of the workforce.** The culture of some groups of employees has been developed over a number of years. In the UK's coal-mining communities, the culture proved almost impossible to change, as it had evolved over a number of generations.

- **The extent to which the organisation's structure reinforces the culture.** A role culture may be difficult to change if emphasis is given to hierarchy and position. It may be necessary to change the structure to change the culture.

- **Informal communication.** If the operation of the business allows employees the opportunity to communicate informally, the existing culture is likely to be reinforced.

It is doubtful whether a business's culture can be changed significantly in the short term. A key factor may be the extent to which the factors determining the strength of the culture can be affected by management action. Changing an organisation's culture may require the business's structure to be reorganised, the hiring of new employees and perhaps new policies such as empowerment. It is not just the shop-floor employees who have to change, but also the management team; the existing culture may be firmly embedded here too.

> **Typical mistake**
>
> Too many students are unsure exactly what is meant by the term 'culture' and many have little understanding of the degree of difficulty in changing a business's culture.

The importance of organisational culture

Revised

It can be argued that a successful business focuses on the behaviour of its employees. If employees have the right attitudes and behave in the desired manner, the business will flourish. Thus, managing the corporate culture is believed by many managers to be a vital element of commercial success.

To some extent this argument might be true. For most businesses and particularly those in a changing environment, developing the appropriate culture will be beneficial. It can also enhance the competitiveness of an organisation. Having an appropriate culture may limit conflict and lessen the possibility of industrial disputes. In the long term it may reduce labour turnover and improve employee motivation, once resistance to the change in culture has been overcome. Changing the culture of an organisation can make the business more innovative, encouraging the development of new, modern products. All of these factors enhance competitive performance.

However, other factors are important determinants of a business's competitiveness, such as exchange rates, interest rates and government economic policies. Similarly, the actions of competitors (e.g. introducing new, advanced products) will affect the competitiveness of firms. Finally, the public's perception of the business will also play a role in determining competitiveness.

> **Now test yourself**
>
> 5 Why does having the 'right' culture contribute towards making a business competitive?
>
> **Answers on p. 112**
>
> Tested

Making strategic decisions

The significance of information management

Revised

Information management is the collection and management of information from one or more sources in the organisation, and the distribution of that information to the relevant employees.

Businesses might need to manage a range of information, including:

- data relating to costs of production and other financial aspects of the business
- marketing information relating to sales, market growth, competitors' actions and changes in consumer tastes
- operations data, such as capacity utilisation, availability of resources used in production and quality performance data
- HR data on labour turnover, wage costs and labour productivity

Most of the information on this list is numerical in form. However, businesses also need qualitative data which, for example, explain customers' attitudes to the business and its brands or products.

Businesses need to collect the right information, to collate and analyse it, and to make it available to the right people in an organisation at the right time. Information helps managers to make decisions at all levels within the organisation.

- **Strategic decisions.** Information is perhaps most necessary before long-term and important decisions are taken. The process of planning is highly dependent on having the right information to hand. For example, information on relevant costs in different countries will help corporate planning, such as a decision on locating a new production facility.
- **Marketing and other functional decisions.** A business will need up-to-date and accurate information on costs, recent sales, competitors' actions and, most importantly, consumers' needs if it is to supply the market with the right products in the right place and at the right price.
- **Tactical decisions.** Even for a relatively simple decision, such as whether to increase production of a product over the next few days, relevant information is essential. Managers will need information on the actual level of orders, the staff that are available and stocks of other resources required.

A well-managed business will manage its information efficiently. This means that it is available promptly to the people who need it, is up to date and is in a form that can be readily understood.

> **information management** — the collection and management of information from one or more sources in the organisation, and the distribution of that information to the relevant employees

Now test yourself

6 Draw a spider chart to illustrate the risks involved in taking strategic decisions without having the maximum amount of information available.

Answers on p. 112

Tested

Approaches to decision making

Revised

It is entirely possible for managers to make even the most important decisions on the basis of a hunch or intuition. This might lead a manager to take a decision that is not supported by the data that are available, or which is not a standard or expected decision in the circumstances. Some managers believe that really great decisions are made by hunches.

Exam practice answers and quick quizzes at **www.therevisionbutton.co.uk/myrevisionnotes**

However, other managers use models and/or theories to take a more scientific approach to decision making.

Ansoff's matrix

This matrix (Figure 8.1) is a framework for considering the relationship between marketing and overall strategy. The technique considers product and market growth and analyses the degree of risk attached to the range of options open to the business. Key findings of Ansoff's matrix are:

- Staying with what you know (e.g. market penetration) represents relatively little risk.

- Moving into new markets with new products is a high-risk strategy.

Assessment is made of the value of each option.

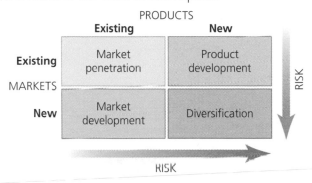

Figure 8.1 Ansoff's matrix

Porter's strategic matrix

Michael Porter of the Harvard Business School is one of the foremost business writers in the world today. One of his best-known contributions to management thinking is his strategic matrix (Figure 8.2). Its purpose is to assist managers in assessing strategy. It assesses whether the business is aiming at producing low-cost or differentiated products. Simultaneously, it judges whether the business is operating in a niche or a mass market.

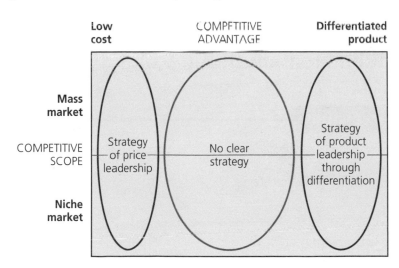

Figure 8.2 Porter's strategic matrix

The fundamental point of Porter's theory is that, whether operating in a niche or a mass market, a business should aim either to be a low-cost producer or to sell a product that is highly differentiated from those of rivals. It should not allow its strategy to drift towards the middle of the matrix, seeking neither price nor product leadership.

Influences on corporate decision making

There are a number of factors that can influence the process of corporate decision making:

- **The business's history.** The business's strategic decisions will be shaped by its history to a greater or lesser extent. If, for example, a business has a history of supplying unusual and innovative products, its senior managers will take this into account when making important decisions.

- **Competitors' decisions.** It is possible that a business's strategic decisions will have to mirror, or respond in some way to, those taken by its competitors. Thus, if a business's rivals relocate to eastern Europe to reduce costs, the business is likely to make a strategic response, or risk losing price competitiveness.

- **The economic environment.** A positive economic environment (steady economic growth, low inflation, stable exchange rates, etc.) may encourage corporate planners and decision-makers to take more risky decisions: for example, in developing new products or expanding into new markets.

- **Technological developments.** Advances in technology can have a considerable impact on the processes of production and therefore may encourage strategic decision-makers to replace labour with technology or to decide to locate in countries with higher wage costs, but access to better support for technological production.

- **Corporate image.** A business might take strategic decisions intended to promote a positive corporate image. This may, for example, entail senior managers taking decisions intended to project the business as environmentally friendly.

> **Examiner's tip**
>
> There are many possible influences on a business's strategic planning. This section considers only a few of the possibilities. You should consider the scenario to which any examination question relates and seek to identify the most relevant ones, rather than simply relying on this list.

Implementing and managing change

Techniques to manage change successfully

Using a project plan

A project plan for use in a change programme entails a number of stages:

Initiation stage

The opening elements of the plan should state what the project needs to accomplish: that is, its aims and objectives.

Making a plan

The people writing the project plan need to decide the following issues:

- What are the strategies and methods to be used to achieve the change objectives?

- What will and will not be covered by the project plan? This is called the **scope and boundaries**.

- What factors are critical to the success of the project?
- Who is going to be involved in the project team and what are their strengths and areas of expertise?
- What budget is available for the plan?
- What are the project outcomes? These can be physical things (tangible deliverables), such as websites, reports and products; or intangible knowledge and experiences.

Work breakdown structure

Any project can be broken down into a set of simpler tasks, which when carried out in sequence will achieve the desired outcome. This process is the **work breakdown structure**. If any task is too complicated to organise easily, it should be broken down into a series of smaller, less complex tasks. Managers can then provide clear instructions about what is to be done, and estimate the time and resources required.

Task allocation

The next stage is to decide who will be responsible for carrying out the individual tasks that have been identified. Task allocation also states when the tasks will be completed to ensure that they are carried out in the right sequence.

Executing the project

Once the project is under way, progress must be reviewed at regular intervals to ensure the project is still on track. Two major elements are used by managers to control their projects:

- **Milestones** — clear targets of what you will deliver by when (short-term goals). If these are not met, managers will need to take corrective action to put the project back on time.
- **Effective communication** — it is essential to have an early warning system for any problems to allow you to take corrective action. All team members should report back regularly on progress, and meetings may be arranged to facilitate this process.

Project evaluation

Evaluating the success of a project plan requires that a number of important questions are answered:

- Were the objectives of the project met?
- Was the outcome of suitable quality, and did it meet the needs of the project's stakeholders?
- Was enough time allocated?
- What lessons did we learn from our mistakes and successes?

Establishing a project team

A successful team is likely to have a number of important characteristics:

- **It should be small and manageable.** Having between four and eight people is best. This will help the team to develop, should allow for a sufficient range of skills, but will lessen the chance of conflict.

Now test yourself

8 Draw a flow chart to illustrate the sequence of key events in implementing a successful project plan.

Answers on p. 112

Tested ☐

- **The team's skills should be complementary.** It should have a range of technical, functional and professional skills appropriate to its task. Well-balanced teams contain people who can approach a task systematically, solve problems, decide on actions, and use appropriate techniques to carry them out.

- **The team must have a common and agreed purpose.** Teams need clearly defined objectives and an agreed timescale. This common purpose will help to focus efforts and to reduce debates and conflict.

- **The team must have the authority to make decisions.** This has the potential to motivate the team, as it offers the opportunity to meet higher-level motivational needs.

- **The team must be accountable for results.** The team must be willing and able to take collective and individual responsibility for their objectives and results.

- **The team must have the necessary resources.** These resources may include staff and finance, as well as physical equipment and research systems on which to base decisions.

- **The team needs a leader.** The leader needs the ability to assess the situation and manage in a number of styles to take the project forward towards the common goal.

Project champions

A **project champion** is a person who has the role of supporting and driving forward a particular project. He or she can play a vital role in managing change projects. Their job is to drive a project forward, advocating its benefits, assisting the team and helping to navigate any problems to keep the project on track.

> **Examiner's tip**
>
> Remember that a successful project team will need a diverse range of skills to enable it to implement change successfully. Training may also be required.

> **project champion** — a person who has the role of supporting and driving forward a particular project

Factors that promote and resist change

Revised

There are a number of factors that can lead to change being resisted:

- **Unclear or unrealistic objectives.** These can result in employees who are implementing change lacking a clear sense of direction and being unable to judge their progress.

- **Uncommitted staff and/or managers.** A time of change is one where employees are often expected to work harder, to work on unfamiliar tasks and to put in additional hours. In such circumstances, any lack of commitment can be serious.

- **Failure to assess risks.** Risk is the chance of something going wrong. Delays can occur which threaten the timely completion of the project. If managers have not allowed for this or have not prepared contingency plans, the success of the entire project may be threatened. Other sources of risk that must be planned for are overspending and the loss of key employees at some stage during the project.

However, there are a number of things that managers of change projects can do to increase the chances of a project succeeding:

- **Give it sufficient resources.** This may refer to money, but equally important will be staffing and providing people with the right skills.

- **Provide training where necessary.** Managers should not assume that members of project teams have all the necessary skills to complete the tasks involved.

- **Allow a realistic timescale.** Project teams should not be placed under too much time pressure to complete the tasks. This can result in poor-quality work and demotivation, and may lead to the failure of the project.

Check your understanding

Tested

1 Distinguish between a merger and a takeover.
2 Define the term 'organisational culture'.
3 How does a contingency plan differ from a corporate plan?
4 Identify one key feature of democratic leadership and one key feature of laissez-faire leadership.
5 State three influences on leadership style.
6 What is a project champion?
7 Explain two factors that are likely to encourage horizontal mergers.
8 Explain why managers might face problems in changing the culture of a business.
9 Why do businesses draw up corporate plans?
10 How might a 'project champion' help a business to implement a successful programme of change management?

Answers on p. 112

Exam practice

Essays

1 Until his untimely death in 2011, Steve Jobs — Apple's CEO — was arguably the most important factor in the company's success. To what extent do you agree with the view that a leader is the most important determinant in a business's success? Justify your answer with reference to Apple and/or other businesses with which you are familiar. [40]

2 People are the most important element in implementing change management successfully and the strongest force opposing it. Do you agree with this statement? Justify your answer with reference to businesses with which you are familiar. [40]

Answers and quick quiz online

Online

Answers

Chapter 1

Now test yourself

1 Diversification. Finance may need to raise capital to fund diversification; operations may set an objective of innovation to produce a wider range of products; marketing may need to adopt objectives to break into a new market (possibly involving greater primary market research); human resources managers might need to recruit additional staff or invest in training existing employees.

2 Profit maximisation. Finance may set an objective of cost minimisation; operations may seek to increase efficiency to assist in cost reduction; marketing may have an objective of increasing market share; human resources might aim to make full use of the workforce's resources (to minimise labour costs).

Check your understanding

1 An objective is a goal or target set by a business at corporate or functional level.

A strategy is a medium- to long-term plan to achieve an objective.

2 A corporate objective is a goal or target for the entire business, e.g. growth.

A functional objective is the goal that is pursued by the particular function within the business.

3 To ensure that the achievement of the functional objective will contribute to the fulfilment of the business's corporate objectives. For example, a marketing department may set an objective of entering new markets to assist the business in meeting its corporate objective of growth.

4 Objectives can operate as clear targets for employees at all levels within the business. Authority can be delegated more easily if junior employees know the targets that they are pursuing when making decisions.

5 The operations department will need to set objectives around research and development to ensure that new products (or processes) can be developed.

The finance department may have to set an objective of managing cash flow carefully to ensure that cash is available to finance research and development.

Chapter 2

Now test yourself

1 Vickers shipbuilders and engineers is likely to have a much longer cash cycle as it can take years to win an order for a ship, and design and build it before receiving full payment. The company may be paid by customers in instalments but will be likely to have to manage its cash flow carefully to ensure it does not run out of cash.

Greggs may face cash-flow problems, but this is less likely as it produces and sells its products within a few days. Further, most of its customers will pay cash.

2 **Cash-flow targets.** External factor: sales are declining in the market, reducing cash inflows. Internal factor: the business has a recent history of overtrading.

Cost minimisation. External factor: demand in the market is price elastic. Internal factor: managers receive bonuses based on profit targets.

ROCE targets. External factor: profits have declined in recent years. Internal factor: the business has an objective of growth and needs funds for reinvestment.

Shareholders' returns. External factor: rival businesses are achieving better returns for their shareholders. Internal factor: the business wishes to attract further investment by shareholders to finance plans to enter new markets.

3 Gross profit is calculated by deducting the cost of goods sold from the business's sales revenue.

Operating profit will be a smaller figure for a specific business in a given year as it is effectively gross profit less expenses and overheads.

Profit for the year may be a lower figure if further deductions in the form of net finance income and taxation have to be made from the operating profit figure.

4 (a) Whether or not to go ahead with a major investment

Gearing ratio	To decide whether or not it can borrow some of the funds required.
Dividend yield ratio	This shows the percentage returns to shareholders and therefore the attractiveness of new share issues.

(b) Assessing a firm's financial success

Current ratio	To judge its short-term financial position and its ability to pay debts as they fall due.
ROCE	This will judge the efficiency of the business at converting capital used in the business into operating profits.

5 Your diagram should include factors such as the following:

- **Finance.** This should increase the business's profit margins and ROCE. It may help to ease cash-flow problems, although this depends on price levels.

- **Marketing.** There will be implications for pricing, the style and type of advertising and the likely product range supplied by the business.

- **Operations.** The business may ask other companies to carry out some of its operations to reduce costs such as cleaning, or it may move them overseas (its call centre, for example). Operations may be simplified, such as an airline only flying one type of plane to make maintenance less expensive.

- **HR.** More use may be made of temporary and part-time workers. Migrant workers may be employed and training costs may be minimised.

Check your understanding

1 A financial objective is a goal or target pursued by the finance department (or function) within an organisation.

A financial strategy is a medium- to long-term plan designed to achieve the objectives of the finance function or department of a business.

2 Internal factors: corporate objectives, nature of the product, and senior managers' attitudes and aspirations.

External factors: competitors' actions, state of the markets and the availability of external finance.

3 Assets are items owned by a business. Examples are property (a non-current asset) and cash (a current asset).

Liabilities are owed by a business to its owners or investors. Liabilities include shareholders' equity and long-term bank loans (a non-current liability).

4 Depreciation is the loss in value of a business's assets over time.

5 The asset turnover ratio, inventory turnover, debtors' collection period and creditors' collection period ratios.

6 The current ratio and the acid test ratio.

7 A profit centre is an area, department, division or branch of an organisation that is allowed to control itself separately from the larger organisation.

8 Payback = £100,000 ÷ £12,500 = 8 years exactly

9 Average annual profit = £1,000,000 ÷ 4 = £250,000

ARR = £250,000 × 100 ÷ £2,000,000 = 12.5%

10 If a business has too little working capital available, it may not be able to finance its day-to-day operations such as purchasing inventories. Too much working capital can also be a problem, as assets such as inventories do not generate profits for a business (and may incur costs such as storage).

11 Profit quality measures the extent to which an individual profit source is sustainable. It is important because businesses naturally seek to earn high-quality profit which means that they can expect to earn it in the future. A one-off source of profit will boost this year's figures only and further actions will be needed if future profits are not to decline.

12 Comparisons with figures for earlier years help us to judge whether a business is performing better than in the past. Comparisons with rivals help us to judge how financially effective a business is in terms of other similar organisations that face similar market conditions.

13 My opinion is that it excludes non-financial information and that it is historical (particularly important in volatile markets). However, there are other possible answers that would be equally correct.

14 **HR.** It is likely to increase training needs, may require recruitment of suitably skilled staff and could lead to increased labour turnover if employees feel threatened by it.

Marketing. It could lead to improved market research based on local 'branches', a wider product range and greater market share if successful.

Operations. It may lead to greater diseconomies of scale if communication problems arise. Products could become less standard as they have to meet the needs of different markets, but this may result in higher quality if customers' needs are met more fully.

15 Quite simply it is best because it takes into account the timing of payments and receipts and the profitability of the investment. Payback ignores profitability and ARR does not take into account the timings of payments and receipts.

Chapter 3

Now test yourself

1 Answers will depend on when this task is tackled, but at the time of writing the following factors may apply:

- **Internal factors.** The company is seeking growth, as is indicated by its moves into overseas markets and different product markets. The business is financially strong — its profits were £3.8 billion in 2010/11 — allowing heavy investment in marketing and positive objectives.

- **External factors.** Many western countries are forecast to have slow growth over the next 2 years and so Tesco's marketing objectives may focus on expansion in developing markets such as China. The supermarket's high market share in groceries in the UK may mean it has to continue to focus on developing market share in non-food markets.

2 **The temperature in the UK.** A positive correlation may be expected here as sales rise in hot weather — although many consumers may buy the lotion for overseas holidays, making the UK temperature irrelevant.

Income levels in the UK. Rising incomes may be expected to have a positive correlation as well, as more people may holiday overseas in hot countries where suntan lotion is essential.

3

Year	Sales value £m	Calculation	Moving average £m
2006	12.8	–	–
2007	11.6	35.5 ÷ 3	11.8
2008	11.1	32.7 ÷ 3	10.9
2009	10.0	33.3 ÷ 3	11.1
2010	12.2	35.6 ÷ 3	11.9
2011	13.4	39.0 ÷ 3	13.0
2012	13.4	–	–

4 (a) **Market development.** Income levels are rising rapidly in overseas markets (China?); market research identifies new segment for existing product; existing markets are saturated.

(b) **Product development.** Sales of existing products are falling; competitors are bringing out new products; company has operational strategy of innovation; existing markets are saturated.

Check your understanding

1 A marketing strategy is the medium- to long-term plan required to achieve a business's marketing objectives.

Marketing objectives are medium- to long-term targets that may provide a sense of direction to the marketing department and to the whole business.

2 Decisions based on hunches or instinct.

Scientific marketing decisions.

3 Extrapolation analyses the past performance of a variable such as sales and extends the trend into the future. The success of extrapolation as a forecasting technique depends upon the future being the same as the past. In volatile markets this is unlikely.

Year	Sales value £m	Calculation	Moving average £m
1	4.0	–	–
2	5.0	14.2 ÷ 3	4.7
3	5.2	16.8 ÷ 3	5.6
4	6.6	19.1 ÷ 3	6.4
5	7.3	–	–

5 Market penetration, market development, product development and diversification.

6 The business's marketing objectives.

The elements of the marketing mix which may be deployed.

The timescale over which the plan is to be implemented.

The results of the business's market analysis.

The resources available, including a marketing budget.

7 A business's managers can use a marketing plan to monitor and amend their performance in terms of marketing actions.

Plans can result in managers becoming inflexible and not taking sensible marketing decisions if they are not part of the plan.

8 Diversification means that a business is unfamiliar with the market in which it is selling and may not have a clear understanding of its customers or the strengths and weaknesses of its rivals. The business will also be selling new products which may be familiar to potential customers and they may not buy them in sufficient quantities.

9 If a business has expansive marketing objectives such as a major programme of product development, its marketing budget will reflect this in terms of resources — the marketing budget will be large to finance market research and promotional activities, for example. In contrast, more modest objectives will require fewer resources.

10 If competitors spend heavily on promotion or PR, it is likely that the business will seek to respond to avoid losing market share and adjust its marketing plan accordingly. If a business draws up a new marketing plan (perhaps including the launch of an important new product), this plan will include responses to competitors' likely reactions, such as cutting the prices of their products.

11 IT can be a cheap and convenient way to collect large amounts of data — for example, by use of loyalty cards.

IT can collect data in a form that makes it simple and inexpensive to analyse and present it using relevant software programs.

Speed and relative cheapness are attractive properties of using IT in this way for most businesses.

12 A low-cost marketing strategy aims to undercut rivals in terms of price by keeping costs of production to a minimum. This can be highly effective in markets where demand is price elastic. A marketing strategy based upon differentiation allows the development of a USP and allows a business to charge higher prices for products that are different in some way from those of its rivals. In effect, this can make demand more price inelastic.

Chapter 4

Now test yourself

1 Cost targets are important in the airline industry and the package holiday industry because demand for these products is price elastic and unit cost targets are important.

Volume targets will be important in manufacturing basic foodstuffs such as tinned beans because this will help firms to spread the high fixed costs of manufacturing over a large volume of output, decreasing unit costs and enhancing competitiveness.

2 GlaxoSmithKline plc, a large UK pharmaceutical company, would benefit from economies of scale in that increasing its size spreads the fixed costs of researching and developing new medicines and lowers the unit cost.

Economies of scale may be less relevant to Rolls-Royce plc, the luxury car manufacturer, which focuses on quality and maintains its exclusivity by producing a low volume of output.

3 **Marketing.** This might require heavy expenditure on promotion to advise customers of new products and to develop brand loyalty.

Finance. The company may have to set challenging ROCE objectives to ensure it generates sufficient funds to invest in future R&D programmes.

Operations. The company may set itself quality targets to ensure satisfaction among its consumers (and possibly to justify its high prices).

4 It can use break even to identify the site requiring the lowest level of output to break even. This may be the most profitable site.

5 Advantages: increased motivation and productivity, enhanced quality, increased sales revenue.

Disadvantages: initial costs of training employees, possibility of redundancies, potential opposition to changes.

6 To reduce costs of production and thereby increase profits.

To enhance quality by producing products to meet the precise needs of each of its customers.

To improve motivation of employees and possibly reduce labour turnover.

Check your understanding

1 A quality product is one that meets customers' needs fully.

2 Efficiency occurs when a business produces the maximum quantity of output using a minimum quantity of inputs.

3 Reducing carbon emissions.

Reducing or eliminating the use of non-sustainable resources.

4 Innovation is the creation of new ideas and the successful development of products from these ideas.

5 Just-in-time (JIT) manufacturing is a Japanese management philosophy that involves having the right items of the right quality in the right place at the right time.

Lean production describes a range of measures designed to use fewer inputs and resources.

Therefore lean production embraces a wider range of techniques, one of which is just-in-time manufacturing.

6 Economies of scale exist when unit costs of production fall as output is increased.

Diseconomies of scale are the financial disadvantages that result from producing on a larger scale, which result in higher unit costs of production.

Therefore they both relate to the effect on unit costs of increasing the scale of production, but describe opposite effects.

7 If a business wishes to reduce its unit costs of production in the long term.

If a business faces inconsistent patterns of demand and needs to be flexible in its levels of production over time.

To produce large quantities of standard products.

8 The innovative product may fail. This means that firms spend enormous sums of money on projects that do not generate any returns.

Other firms may copy the idea. This can be a major problem for a business that has incurred all the research and development costs without getting the benefits of selling large numbers of premium-priced products.

9 It allows a business to be closer to its markets and to monitor market trends better.

It permits large businesses to operate as several smaller businesses, gaining economies of scale without incurring diseconomies of scale.

Multi-site location encourages a greater degree of delegation and empowerment, which can enhance motivation and employee performance.

10 Some activities (such as building the Olympic Park in Stratford) may be too complex to represent on a network.

It is notoriously difficult to calculate durations of activities accurately, which calls into doubt the whole worth of the technique.

This is only the starting point of managing a project successfully — much else needs to be done.

Chapter 5

Now test yourself

1 Growth — matching the workforce to the business's needs as the business will wish to meet customers' demands promptly.

Price-inelastic demand — maintaining good employer–employee relations to assist a business in attracting high-calibre employees and to supply high-quality products, enabling the setting of premium prices.

Highly complex product — making the full use of the workforce's potential to supply products that meet customers' needs fully.

2 The business will need to start by forecasting sales and therefore its future need for labour. It should then consider the labour force it possesses currently and changes expected in this due to retirements. At this point it can plan how to convert its current labour force into its required one, using techniques such as recruitment and redeployment.

3 Matrix structure: well-trained staff, innovative culture, operating in a rapidly changing environment, a need for the organisation to be highly flexible and responsive.

Functional hierarchical structure: traditional culture and market in which customers are seeking traditional products, a very large business.

4 If workforces are generally highly skilled, if communication is weak, if an organisation has high labour costs as a proportion of total costs (relative to competitors), if employees are trained in advance of the programme of delegation or if it has an excessive number of levels of hierarchy.

Check your understanding

1 Human resource objectives are the targets pursued by the HR function or department of the business. Examples are:

- matching the workforce to the needs of the business
- making full use of the workforce's potential

2 Internal influences: corporate objectives and the types of product.

External influences: price elasticity of demand for the product and corporate image.

3 A hard HR strategy views employees as a resource to be used as efficiently as possible. Employees are hired as cheaply as possible, managed closely and made redundant when no longer required.

A soft HR strategy is based on the belief that employees are a business's most valuable asset. Employees are valued and developed, and help to make a business competitive.

4 A workforce plan sets out a business's future labour needs and details how these will be met.

5 Details of the business's current workforce, its size, skills, locations and age profile.

An analysis of likely changes in the demand for the business's products and the business's future labour requirements.

6 Employees may be given part-time and temporary contracts, allowing the business to respond efficiently to changes in the level of demand for its products.

Outsourcing. This is the use of other firms to supply part of their output during periods of heavy demand.

7 Centralisation occurs when the majority of decisions are the responsibility of just a few people at the top of the organisation.

Decentralisation occurs when control shifts sideways or horizontally, between people at the same level in the organisation.

In many senses, centralisation is the opposite of delegation.

8 Arbitration resolves a dispute by appointing an independent person or panel to decide on a way of settling the dispute. Conciliation is a method of resolving individual or collective disputes in which a neutral third party encourages the continuation of negotiation rather than industrial action. The key distinction is that an arbitrator has more power to take decisions to resolve disputes.

9 ACAS's main responsibility is to prevent or resolve industrial disputes.

It also advises employers, trade unions and employers' associations on topics such as reducing absenteeism, employee sickness and payment systems.

It aims to improve business practices to reduce the possibility of industrial disputes.

10 This occurs when a business takes a decision to no longer recognise a trade union in the workplace. The Employment Relations Act (2000) has made it more difficult for employers to derecognise trade unions. It grants unions the right to recognition as long as they have over 50% of the workforce as members.

Chapter 6

Now test yourself

1 Shareholders may support it as lower costs may lead to higher long-term profits.

Employees are likely to oppose it because of loss of jobs.

Consumers may support it as it can result in lower prices, although others may oppose it ethically because of the job losses.

Suppliers are likely to be against it because they may lose orders.

The government is likely to oppose it, not least because of the loss of tax revenue.

Check your understanding

1 A corporate strategy is a medium- to long-term plan through which a business intends to achieve its corporate objectives.

2 Corporate objectives are medium- to long-term goals established to coordinate the business.

Marketing objectives are medium- to long-term targets that provide a sense of direction to the marketing department or function.

The difference is that the former relate to the whole business and the latter to a single function — marketing.

3 Having a positive image can help to increase sales if consumers view the business favourably.

It can avoid the need for price cuts, which may result in lower profits.

It can take some time to recover from incidents that may damage a company's reputation.

Chapter 7

Now test yourself

1 A business may enjoy rising sales. This is more likely if it sells luxury products and may allow it to increase its prices and therefore its profit margins.

Government spending may rise on infrastructure projects such as new roads, offering work for businesses and helping to reduce costs of production by, for example, improving the transport network.

2 Answers may include the following:
- The cost of hiring workers may increase as fewer workers are unemployed.
- The business may replace more expensive workers with machinery.
- Sales may increase because more people are in work and therefore earning wages and buying products.
- The business may seek new employees overseas.

3 The flow chart should contain the following sequence:
- A rise in interest rates leads to an increase demand for pounds by overseas investors.
- The price of pounds (the exchange rate) rises.
- Exports become more expensive overseas.
- Sales fall as a consequence, depending on price elasticity of demand.

4 (a) The price of exports overseas will fall.
   (b) The price of imports will fall.
   (c) The price of exports will rise.

5 Businesses in emerging markets may be able to produce more cheaply than established UK producers.

Rationalisation may permit a business to divert resources into producing products in which they have a competitive advantage.

Rationalisation may also remove excess capacity, enabling a UK business to become more price competitive.

6 The diagram might include the following:
- It will increase the level of economic activity.
- Businesses may borrow and invest more.
- Consumers may reduce savings and increase spending, especially on luxury products.
- The exchange rate of the currency may fall, making exports cheaper and boosting sales.
- Imports will become more expensive, improving the price competitiveness of UK businesses.

7 Shareholders: financial returns in the form of dividends and higher share prices.

Managers: high wages and a clear career path.

Employees: job security and jobs that motivate.

Suppliers: regular orders and prompt payment.

The government: job creation and stable tax receipts.

Local residents: avoidance of pollution and employment prospects.

8 It may enable the business to reduce its costs and increase its profit margins.

It may operate policies that make it appear to meet its social responsibilities, while ignoring them in reality.

It may feel that there is little competitive advantage to be gained from such an approach if rivals behave similarly.

9 Should a business train its own employees rather than 'poaching' ready-trained workers from a rival business?

Should a distributor accept a profitable contract to transport tobacco products, knowing that they damage consumers' health?

10 Small firms may not believe that the investment required will produce reasonable returns.

Businesses in 'non-polluting' industries may argue that little advantage will arise from their use.

Some managers may be unaware of their potential benefits.

11 Many manufacturers of foods promote traditional 'handmade' products.

Airlines may operate call centres to book flights rather than using websites.

Check your understanding

1 This refers to the amount of production, expenditure and employment in the economy.

2 Ethics can be defined as a code of behaviour considered morally correct. Taking an ethical decision means doing what is morally right.

3 A social audit is an independent investigation into a firm's activities and its impact on society.

4 It may lead to lower sales in the retailer's outlets, especially if it sells luxury and high-price products.

The retailer may be able to hire employees at lower wage rates, as there are greater numbers of unemployed people available.

5 The price of one currency expressed in terms of another, for example £1 = $1.60.

6 The cost of its imports of raw materials will rise as a result of the fall in the exchange rate.

The price of its exports could be cheaper, which, if demand is price elastic, will result in higher sales and increased revenue.

7 Globalisation refers to the trend for many markets to become worldwide in scope.

8 Increased sales of products as consumers' incomes rise in these markets (and possibly higher prices over time).

The possibility of establishing low-cost production facilities in these countries, thereby enhancing price competitiveness.

9 Fiscal policy refers to government policies based on taxation and its own expenditure.

Monetary policy centres on adjusting the amount of money in circulation and hence the level of spending and economic activity.

The latter involves altering the cost, the amount of money in the economy, while the former relates to the balance of the government's budget.

10 It will increase the cost of borrowing, therefore reducing the amount of investment undertaken by businesses, lowering employment and expenditure.

Consumer spending will also fall as consumers save more, attracted by higher interest rates.

Consumers will also be less willing to borrow to purchase expensive items such as houses and cars.

11 Fewer accidents may take place, meaning fewer absences among employees, which would help to maintain productivity levels.

Motivation may be enhanced due to the existence of these laws, which help to ensure that employees' security needs (as identified by Maslow) are met.

12 In highly competitive markets, the implementation of an ethical policy may act as a USP, providing differentiation and allowing demand to become more price inelastic.

Small businesses competing against larger rivals may use this, as they cannot compete on price.

Some entrepreneurs may have a genuine desire to operate businesses in which only morally correct decisions are taken.

13 New entrants to the market increasing supply when demand may not be changing.

The establishment of a dominant business, which may drive other businesses out of the market.

Falling demand in a market, meaning that existing businesses are competing for a reduced number of customers.

14 It may be if it leads to higher levels of demand and possibly higher prices.

It may cause inflation (if it results in an economic boom), which can make UK businesses less price competitive on world markets.

Thus, it depends on the circumstances.

15 They may mean that businesses have to shed labour. Redundancies can be costly and damage a business's corporate image

It may increase costs to purchase new capital equipment and provide appropriate training for employees.

It may place businesses under continual pressure to implement a programme of new product development based on the technological change.

Chapter 8

Now test yourself

1 **Customers** may benefit from lower prices as a result of economies of scale, or suffer a reduction in choice.

Employees may be disadvantaged in that jobs are likely to be lost as the merger or takeover may involve rationalisation. Employees may also be redeployed.

The government may suffer from a reduction in tax revenue if a consequence is that part of the business relocates overseas (as in the case of Kraft's takeover of Cadbury).

Shareholders might benefit, in the short term at least, if share prices rise.

2 A decline in profits or profitability (profit margin or ROCE).

Falling labour productivity and/or significant increases in labour turnover.

A steady decline in market share and/or decline in brand recognition.

3 The diagram should include factors such as the following:
   - when markets are changing over time
   - when a business is becoming steadily less competitive
   - at a time of great change such as a recession
   - following the appointment of a new chief executive or a merger

4 Clear, effective management with purpose and vision.

Support for the change from key personnel within the company.

Sufficient funds allocated to training.

Allowing a reasonable timescale during which the change will take place.

5   It may enable a business to use its employees as efficiently as possible — a person-orientated culture may improve the quality of a business's products if employees are empowered.

This may assist a business in meeting its customers' needs — for example, a task culture to be more creative.

A power culture may be suitable for a high-risk environment where decision making and entrepreneurship are of great importance.

6   The chart might contain the following information:

- Marketing risks are substantial and include misunderstanding consumers' needs or market growth rates or competitors' actions.

- Financial risks occur if the business is not familiar with its position with regard to cash and profits, and has failed to prepare financial forecasts.

- Operational risks may occur if the firm does not research likely sales and match them to available capacity.

- Workforce planning will be an integral part of taking strategic decisions — without this the business may not have the right-size workforce with the required skills.

7   **The business's scale.** A large business may benefit from economies of scale and be able to choose to produce at low cost, while a smaller business may have to opt for a differentiation strategy.

Corporate objectives. For example, an objective of growth might encourage the adoption of a low-cost strategy to maximise sales and market share.

Whether the business operates in a niche or a mass market. Businesses in a niche market may be more likely to differentiate (to meet the precise needs of the niche) and may charge premium prices.

8   The flow chart should contain the following stages:

- Initiation stage
- Drawing up the outline plan
- Providing details on the plan — the work breakdown structure
- Task allocation
- Executing the project
- Evaluating the project

Check your understanding

1   A merger is the combining of two or more firms into a single business following agreement by the firms' management teams and shareholders.

A takeover occurs when one company acquires complete control of another by purchasing over 50% of its share capital.

2   An organisation's culture is the attitudes, ideas and beliefs that are shared by its employees.

3   A corporate plan is a long-term strategy by which a business hopes to achieve its corporate objectives. This type of planning involves matching the corporate objectives to the resources available.

A contingency plan is designed to deal with an adverse event which may damage the business's well-being.

4   Democratic leadership encourages participation by junior employees, which can have positive effects on motivation levels and performance.

Laissez-faire management leads to uncoordinated delegation and therefore relies strongly on the skills of junior employees if it is to be effective.

5   The nature of the task.

The personality and skills of the leader.

Takeovers and mergers.

6   A project champion is a person who has the role of supporting and driving forward a particular project.

Their job is to drive a project forward, advocating its benefits, assisting the team and helping to navigate any problems to keep the project on track.

Seb Coe is an example of a project champion in relation to the London 2012 Olympics.

7   A horizontal merger is the joining together of two firms in the same industry and at the same stage of production.

If an industry benefits from significant economies of scale, firms will merge to try and reduce their unit costs of production.

If demand in a market is price elastic, this will encourage horizontal mergers to help firms to use scale to become more price competitive.

8   If informal communication in the organisation is operating on a wide scale and participants in this communication oppose the change.

In organisations with very low levels of labour turnover, large numbers of long-serving employees may oppose the change in culture.

Ineffective action by managers who do not plan carefully and implement changes such as introducing a suitable organisational structure as part of the process.

9   To give the entire business a sense of purpose and direction.

To provide guidance to the functional areas of the business, such as HR, when drawing up functional plans.

To encourage managers to be forward looking and proactive.

10   He or she can play a vital role in literally 'championing' the change process.

They may be inspirational and motivational, and thereby influence the actions of others.

They may play a key role in PR and marketing, and help to attract support and financial resources.